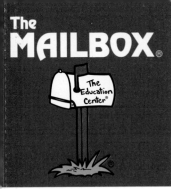

The MAILBOX®
The Education Center®

Learning Centers

Our best learning center ideas from the 1995–2004 issues of *The Mailbox®* magazine

- **Phonics**
- **Grammar & Sentence Skills**
- **Writing**
- **Math**
- **Reading Comprehension**
- **Social Studies**

And Much More!

Includes Colorful Ready-to-Go Pieces

Editorial Team: Becky S. Andrews, Kimberley Bruck, Karen P. Shelton, Diane Badden, Thad H. McLaurin, Sharon Murphy, Karen A. Brudnak, Juli Docimo Blair, Hope Rodgers, Dorothy C. McKinney

Production Team: Lori Z. Henry, Pam Crane, Rebecca Saunders, Jennifer Tipton Cappoen, Chris Curry, Sarah Foreman, Theresa Lewis Goode, Greg D. Rieves, Barry Slate, Donna K. Teal, Zane Williard, Tazmen Carlisle, Marsha Heim, Lynette Dickerson, Mark Rainey

www.themailbox.com

©2006 The Mailbox®
All rights reserved.
ISBN10 #1-56234-722-5 • ISBN13 #978-156234-722-2

Manufactured in the United States
10 9 8 7 6 5 4 3 2 1

Table of Contents

Skills Grid

Skill	Phonics	Word Skills & Vocabulary	Grammar & Sentence Skills	Writing	Reading Comprehension	Reference Skills	Number & Operations	Measurement	Geometry	Data Analysis	Social Studies
Language Arts Skills											
onsets and rimes	4										
blends	4										
short and long vowels	5										
prefix re-		11									
suffixes		11									
synonyms		12									
antonyms		12									
homophones		13									
contractions		14									
compound words		15									
spelling		16, 17									
word investigation		17									
sentence building			29								
complete and incomplete sentences			30								
subjects and predicates			30, 31								
capitalization			32								
quotation marks			32								
nouns			33								
common and proper nouns			33								
proper nouns			34								
possessive nouns			34								
plural and possessive nouns			35								
singular and plural nouns			35								
plurals			36								
irregular plurals			36								
pronouns			37								
verbs			38, 39								
adjectives			39								
parts of speech			40								
handwriting				56							
proofreading				56							
creative writing				57, 58, 59							
dialogue writing				59							
descriptive writing				60							
newspaper article				60							
list making				61							
letter writing				62							
classified ad				63							
writing for a purpose				63							
main idea and supporting details					66						
sequencing					66						
facts and opinions					67						
comparing and contrasting					68						
cause and effect					68						
ABC order						70					
guide words						71, 72					
dictionary skills						72					
Math Skills											
odd and even numbers							76				
ordinal numbers							76				
skip-counting							77				
ordering three-digit numbers							77				
place value							78, 79, 80				
addition							78, 80, 81				
fact families							81, 82				
math facts							83, 84, 86				
addition and subtraction							84, 85, 87				
computation							86, 88, 89				
two-digit addition							87				
word problems							88				
multiplication arrays							89				
multiplication facts							90, 91, 92				
division facts							92				
money							93, 94, 95, 96				
fractions							97, 98				
linear measurement								113, 114, 115			
time								116, 117			
shapes									119		
congruency and symmetry									119		
ordered pairs										120	
collecting and recording data										120	
Social Studies Skills											
map skills											122, 123
map and globe skills											123
geography											123, 124
goods and services											124

Phonics

Mouthwatering Words

Dish up refreshing **onset and rime** practice! Label a disposable bowl, as shown, for each listed rime and a Ping-Pong ball (ice cream) for each listed onset. Place the ice cream in a clean, empty ice-cream carton. Set the carton, bowls, an ice-cream scooper, paper, and pencils at a center.

A student divides her paper into fourths and labels each section with a featured rime. She places a scoop of ice cream in a bowl labeled with a rime that forms a word with the onset. Then she writes the word on her paper. In a similar manner, she identifies one more rime that can be used with the onset. Then she repeats the process with the remaining onsets. How tempting!

Laura Hess
Providence School
Waynesboro, PA

Blending Blends

Whip up a batch of **blend** practice in a matter of minutes! Program each of ten yellow construction paper cards with a desired blend. Then, for each yellow card, program two white cards with different word endings. Each word ending must create a word when joined with the blend on the yellow card. Place the programmed cards in a large unbreakable bowl. Store the bowl, a wooden spoon, a baking sheet, a chef's hat, pencils, and a supply of paper at a center. A student uses the wooden spoon to gently stir the paper cards. Then he removes a yellow and a white card from the bowl. If the programming on the cards makes a word, he places the cards on the baking sheet and writes the word on his paper. If a word cannot be formed, he returns the cards to the bowl. The student continues in this manner until he has recorded ten different words on his paper.

adapted from an idea by Melissa Springer
Greenbrier Intermediate
Chesapeake, VA

Word Skills & Vocabulary

Picturing a Prefix

Students will want to return to this vocabulary center again and again! Label individual cards with different words containing the **prefix re-.** Place the cards, a dictionary, paper, pencils, glue, and crayons or markers at a center. A student selects a word card and glues it to the top of a sheet of paper. On the paper he writes a brief definition of the word and then he writes and illustrates a sentence that features it. Display students' work at the center and the meaning of the prefix *re-* is sure to become perfectly clear!

Sue Lorey
Arlington Heights, IL

Clear Endings

Here's a hands-on activity that brings **suffixes** into clear view. For each root word on the answer key shown, label a separate 3" x 5" index card, leaving space after the word. Cut four 3" x 5" rectangles from a blank transparency sheet. Use a permanent marker to write each featured suffix on a different rectangle. Then prepare an answer key. Place the index cards, rectangles, and answer key in a large labeled envelope. Set the envelope at a center with paper and pencils. A student removes the words and suffixes. He positions the suffixes on selected cards to form new words and writes each word on his paper. He adds suffixes to the remaining root words in a similar manner, adding each newly formed word to his paper. Then he checks his work with the answer key.

adapted from an idea by Kish Harris
Southampton Academy
Courtland, VA

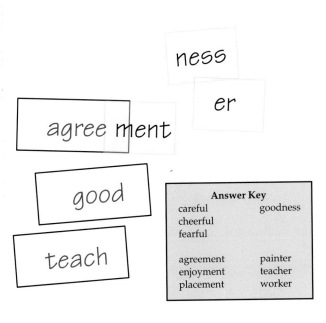

Answer Key	
careful	goodness
cheerful	
fearful	
agreement	painter
enjoyment	teacher
placement	worker

11

Word Skills & Vocabulary

Soaring Synonyms

Students take **synonyms** to new heights with this partner game! Prepare two construction paper kite cutouts and attach a 14-inch length of yarn to each one. Make a construction paper copy of page 19. Cut out the game pieces along the bold lines and store them in a paper lunch bag. Place the bag and kites at a center. Arrange for students to visit the center in pairs.

Each player selects a kite. To take a turn, a player randomly takes a game piece from the bag. If it has a word, he keeps it for later use. If it does not, he sets it aside. When he collects two synonyms, he arranges them on his kite tail to resemble a bow. After all the game pieces have been drawn, players return the blank and unused game pieces to the bag. They continue play until one player has five bows on his kite tail and is declared the winner.

Opposites Attract

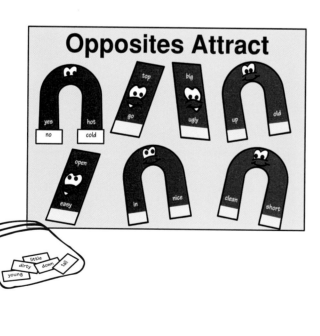

Attract plenty of student interest with this **antonym** center! Copy several construction paper bar and horseshoe patterns from page 18 and cut them out. Add desired details to the cutouts and then glue them to a sheet of poster board titled "Opposites Attract." Attach a small piece of magnetic tape to each magnet pole and write one word of a different antonym pair near the tape. Write the remaining word of each pair on an individual card. Glue a paper clip to the back of each word card and create an answer key for self-checking. Store the cards, the poster, and the answer key at a center. A student attaches each card to its antonym. Then he uses the answer key to check his work.

Alice Fredley
Northumberland Elementary
Heathsville, VA

Word Skills & Vocabulary

Homophone Hives

Create a buzz in your classroom with these **homophone** hives. Duplicate on yellow construction paper a desired number of the beehive patterns on page 20. Label each bee's wings with a pair of homophones; then program the hive with a sentence that incorporates one of the homophones. (Insert a blank in the sentence where the homophone should appear.) Laminate the patterns for durability and cut them out. Next, use a permanent marker to program the back of each hive for self-checking. Store the cutouts in a resealable plastic bag. Place the bag, writing paper, and pencils at a center. A student copies each sentence on his paper, replacing each blank with one of the provided homophones. Then he flips the cut-out to check his work.

Maureen Casazza
Honesdale, PA

sea see

I _____ the dog.

Pairs of Pears

To review **homophones**, use the patterns on page 21 to make ten pear shapes. Program every two pears with a pair of homophones. Cut the shapes, and then program each pair for self-checking. Store the cutouts at a center along with pencils, crayons, and a supply of paper. A student finds a match for each pear; then she flips the cutouts to verify her work. Next, she copies each homophone pair on her paper and writes a sentence that includes the homophones (or forms of them).

Amy Barsanti
Pines Elementary
Roper, NC

flower   flour

stare, stair
My dog sits on the stairs and stares at me!
flour, flower
A flower smells a lot better than a bag of flour.

Word Skills & Vocabulary

Cube of Cards

After your students have played this partner **contraction** game a few times, they'll be eager to make their own versions. To make a Cube of Cards game, label an even number of colorful cards with sets of words that will form contractions. Label the outside of an empty tissue box as shown, and store the cards inside. Place the resulting Cube of Cards game at a center.

To play, each partner draws a card from the cube. If the twosome agrees that the two cards are a match, the cards are set aside and each player draws another card. If the cards do not match, both cards are returned to the cube and play continues. When all of the cards have been matched, the game is over.

Peyton Stooksbury
Briceville Elementary
Lake City, TN

High-Flying Contractions

To prepare, write several **contractions** on individual paper slips and store them in a container. Make several construction paper copies of the bow patterns on page 22. Place the container, a kite template, construction paper, scissors, crayons, pencils, yarn, and glue (or tape) at a center. A student traces one kite shape on construction paper and cuts along the resulting outline. He personalizes and decorates the kite and sets it aside. Next, he selects five contractions from the container. He writes each contraction and its corresponding word pair on a bow cutout; then he glues the bow cutouts at equal intervals along a yarn length. To assemble his kite, he glues the top of his resulting kite string to the bottom of his kite cutout.

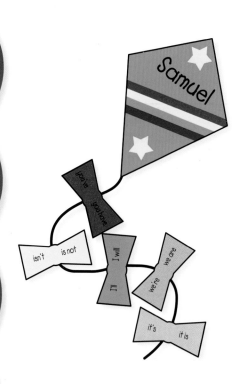

Peggy A. Perry
Pine Tree Elementary School
Center Conway, NH

14

Word Skills & Vocabulary

Banana Splits

Tempt your students to practice **compound words** with this puzzle center! Duplicate several banana patterns from page 25 on construction paper and label each one with two words that, when joined together, form a compound word. Cut out the shapes; then use a different jigsaw style to cut each banana in half. Store the banana pieces in a clean ice-cream container. Place the container, a supply of paper, and pencils at a center. A student removes the cutouts from the container, matches the banana halves to form compound words, and writes the words on her paper.

To extend the center activity, place a dictionary at the center and post the ice-cream code from page 23. Challenge each child to create additional compound words using the programming on the banana halves. After recording the compound words on the back of her paper, she verifies each one with the dictionary. Then she tallies her confirmed compound words, refers to the code, and illustrates at the bottom of her paper the dessert she's earned.

adapted from an idea by Sr. M. Dorothy Salazar
Incarnate Word Academy
Brownsville, TX

Ice-Cream Compound Word Code
1–2 words = 1 scoop
3–5 words = 2 scoops
6–9 words = 3 scoops
10 or more words = banana split!

Chunky Chocolate

Emma
cowboy
hotdog

cow boy
hot dog

Compound Worms

These unique earthworms will have students digging into **compound words!** Make a brown construction paper copy of page 26. Cut out each worm; then cut each worm into two sections. Also cut out the answer key. Place the worm sections in a small pail. Set the pail, answer key, and paper at a center. A student arranges the sections to form ten compound words; she uses the answer key to check her work. Then she chooses five of the compound words and writes a sentence with each one.

Cindy Powell
Erie, PA

rain bow
base ball
oat meal
cake
earth worm
cup

Word Skills & Vocabulary

Spelling Success

Letter manipulatives make this **spelling** idea a favorite. Program one-inch grid paper with the letters in the week's spelling words. (Repeat letters if they are used more than once in a word.) Copy the grid to make a class supply. Place the copies at a center along with the spelling list and a class supply of envelopes. Arrange for students to visit the center in pairs.

Each partner cuts out the letters on her grid and personalizes her envelope. Partner 1 places her letters in her envelope and then sets the envelope aside. To begin, Partner 1 reads aloud the first word on the list; Partner 2 arranges her letters to spell the word. Next, Partner 1 spells the word aloud. Partner 2 checks her spelling, corrects any errors, and then writes the word on her envelope. The partners continue this process with the remaining words. Then they switch roles and repeat the activity. Encourage students to take their letter-filled envelopes home for more hands-on spelling practice!

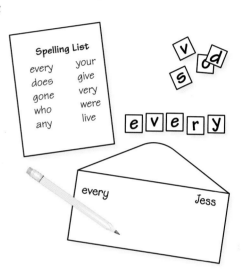

adapted from an idea by Elizabeth Dederich
Westwood Elementary
Springdale, AR

Clip and Spell

Stir up an interest in weekly **spelling** practice at this partner center! Program a spring-type clothespin for each letter of the alphabet. Label extra clothespins for frequently used letters. Store the clothespins and a paint stick in a bucket or a clean and empty paint can; then place the container and a copy of the weekly spelling list at a center. One student becomes the caller, and his partner is the speller. The caller says the first word on the list and then watches closely as his partner spells the word by clipping clothespins onto the paint stick. If the correct spelling is given, the speller removes the clothespins from the paint stick, and the caller reads aloud the next word on the list. If an incorrect spelling is given, the caller repeats the word, and the partners work together to spell it. After each word on the list is correctly spelled, the partners change roles and repeat the activity. Reprogramming the center is a snap—simply replace the spelling list each week.

Amy Ekmark
Eastside Elementary
Lancaster, CA

Word Sleuths

This **word investigation** activity is easy to adapt to your young sleuths' reading needs! Program several cards with grade-appropriate categories of words, such as "long /a/ words" or "compound words." Place the cards, several picture books, and a magnifying glass at a center stocked with paper and pencils. A student chooses a card and copies the category on her paper. She searches the books, using the magnifying glass if desired, to find a designated number of words in the category. She jots the words on her paper and then continues with the remaining cards as time allows. Words have never been more intriguing!

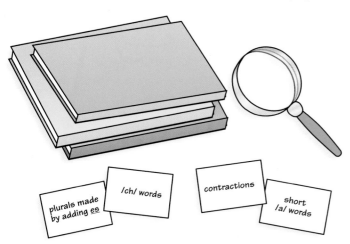

plurals made by adding <u>es</u>

/ch/ words

contractions

short /a/ words

Michelle Yoko-Rosengrant
Wingate Elementary School
Wingate, PA

TEC61024

TEC61024

TEC61024

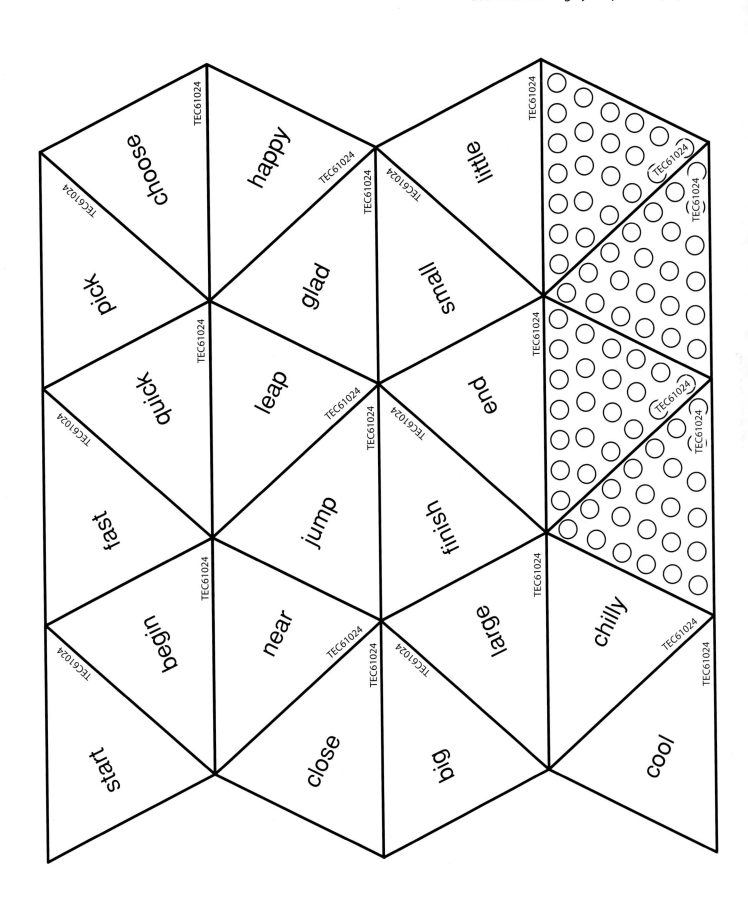

choose

happy

little

pick

glad

small

TEC61024

TEC61024

TEC61024

TEC61024

quick

leap

end

TEC61024

fast

jump

finish

TEC61024

TEC61024

begin

near

large

chilly

TEC61024

TEC61024

start

close

big

cool

TEC61024

TEC61024

Bee Patterns

Use with "Homophone Hives" on page 13.

TEC61024

TEC61024

TEC61024

TEC61024

TEC61024

TEC61024

Kite Bows

Use with "High-Flying Contractions" on page 14.

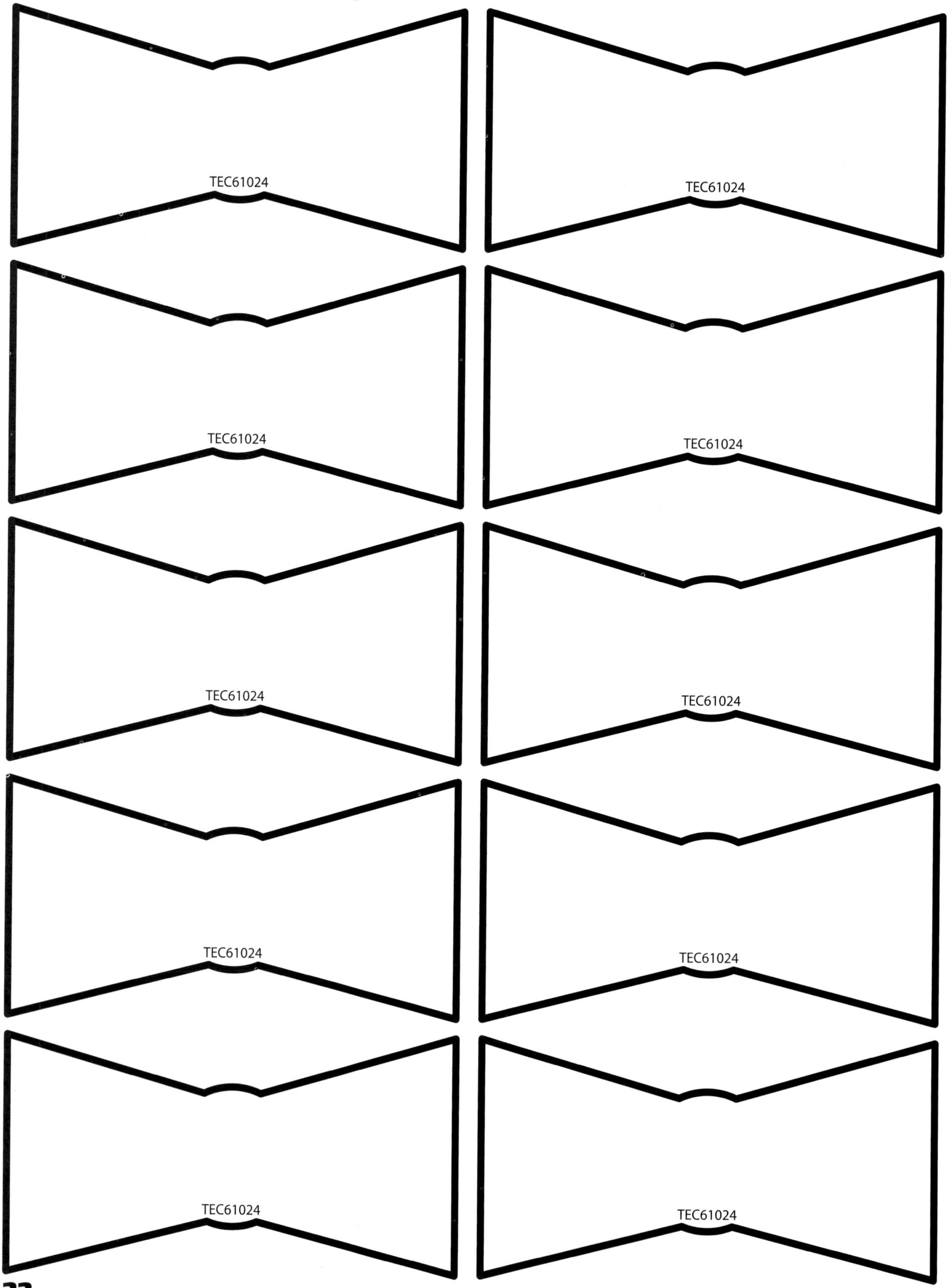

TEC61024

TEC61024

TEC61024

TEC61024

TEC61024

TEC61024

TEC61024

TEC61024

TEC61024

TEC61024

TEC61024

TEC61024

TEC61024

TEC61024

TEC61024

TEC61024

TEC61024

TEC61024

TEC61024

TEC61024

Ice-Cream Compound Word Code

1–2 words = 1 scoop

3–5 words = 2 scoops

6–9 words = 3 scoops

10 or more words =

banana split!

Note to the teacher: Use with "Banana Splits" on page 15.

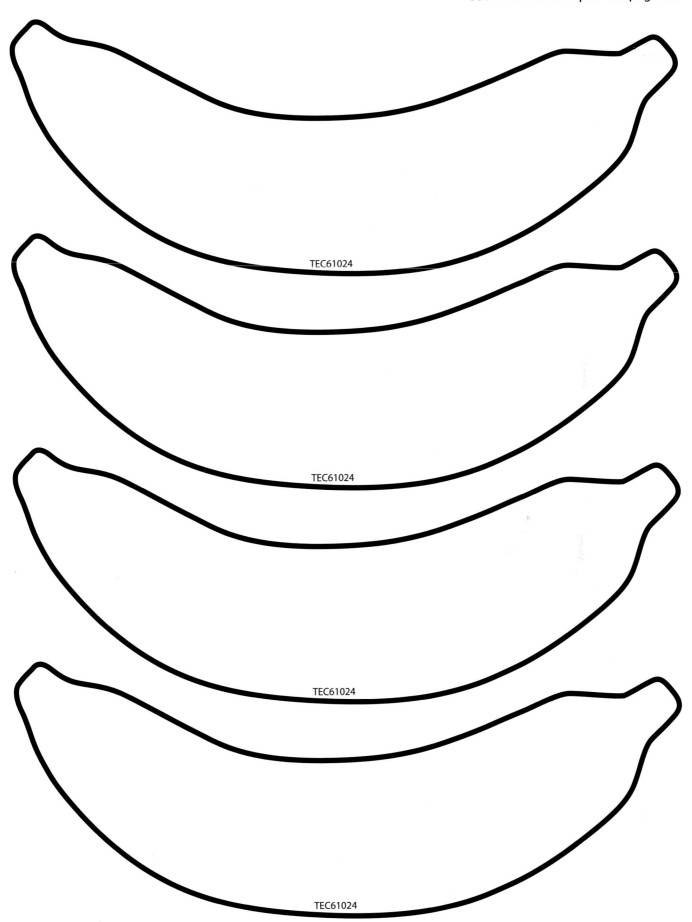

TEC61024

TEC61024

TEC61024

TEC61024

Worm Patterns and Answer Key
Use with "Compound Worms" on page 15.

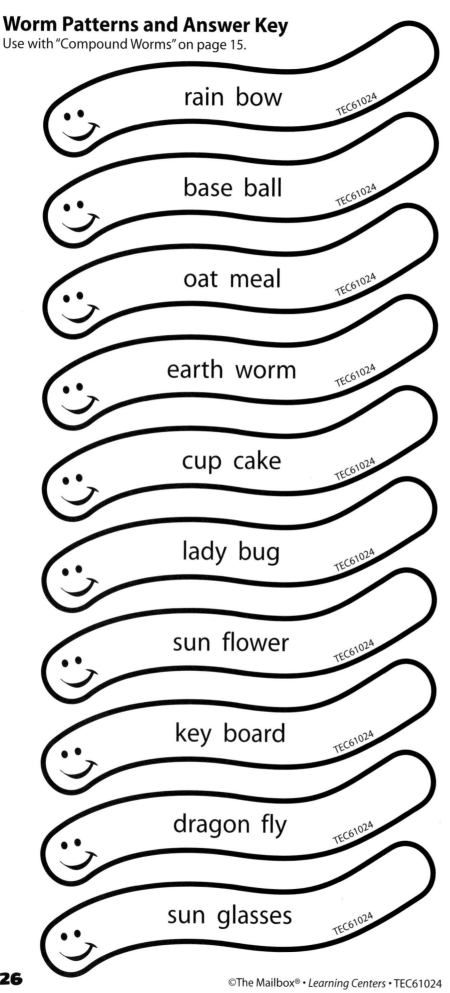

rain bow TEC61024

base ball TEC61024

oat meal TEC61024

earth worm TEC61024

cup cake TEC61024

lady bug TEC61024

sun flower TEC61024

key board TEC61024

dragon fly TEC61024

sun glasses TEC61024

Grammar & Sentence Skills

State-of-the-Art Sentence Builders

Students can show their stuff at this **sentence-building** center. Stock a center with glue, scissors, writing paper, discarded newspapers and magazines, and a copy of the task cards on page 41. A student selects and completes one or more task cards. This activity is a great evaluation tool since students are both identifying and using different parts of speech. And your youngsters are sure to enjoy the hands-on approach to sentence building.

Kym Sitz
Hay Branch Elementary
Killeen, TX

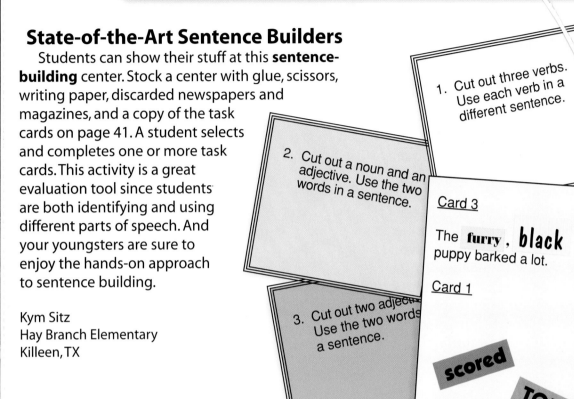

1. Cut out three verbs. Use each verb in a different sentence.

2. Cut out a noun and an adjective. Use the two words in a sentence.

3. Cut out two adjective. Use the two words a sentence.

Card 3

The **furry** , *black* puppy barked a lot.

Card 1

scored

TOLD

screamed

Sentences on the Go

Take **sentence writing** on the road! Cut out the patterns on page 43 and store them in a resealable plastic bag. Place the bag and a supply of writing paper at a center. A student sets the car on a work surface and then places a chosen license plate on it. Next, she reads the license plate letters and writes a noun that begins with the first letter and a verb that begins with the second letter. She pens a sentence with the words and then sets the license plate aside. She repeats the activity as time allows. For a greater challenge, add a letter to each license plate and have students brainstorm adjective-noun-verb combinations for their sentences.

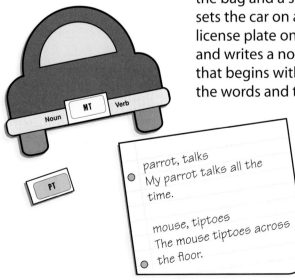

parrot, talks
My parrot talks all the time.

mouse, tiptoes
The mouse tiptoes across the floor.

Laura Hess
Providence School
Greencastle, PA

Grammar & Sentence Skills

Very "Apple-tizing"!

Students get to the core of **complete and incomplete sentences** at this center. Create two large, tree-shaped poster-board cutouts. Label one tree trunk "Complete Sentences" and the other "Incomplete Sentences." Using the patterns on page 45, duplicate a colorful supply of apples. Program the apples with complete and incomplete sentences; then cut them out and label the backs for self-checking. Place the apple cutouts in a basket; then store the basket and the two trees at a center. A student sorts the apples onto the appropriate trees by reading the words written on each apple. When he is finished, he checks his work by turning over the apples.

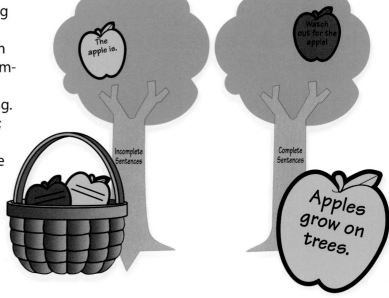

Tonya Byrd
William H. Owen Elementary
Hope Mills, NC

Clip It!

Reviewing **subjects and predicates** is a snap at this easy-to-make center! Program several sentence strips with desired sentences, leaving extra space between the words in each sentence. To program the sentence strips for self-checking, clip a clothespin to each sentence strip to separate the subject and the predicate; then flip the strip over and draw a dot on the back in the corresponding location. Remove and store the clothespins in a decorated container. Then place the strips and the container of clothespins at a center. A student reads each sentence, clips a clothespin onto the strip to separate the subject and the predicate, and flips the strip to check her work.

Holly L. Cable
Page Hilltop School
Ayer, MA

Grammar & Sentence Skills

Subjects and Predicates

What's the best way to sum up this **subject and predicate** activity? Complete sentences! Program separate sentence strips with the provided subject and predicate. Mount and label photos of school personnel and then place the resulting poster, the labeled sentence strips, story paper, pencils, and crayons at a center. A student writes a complete sentence by copying and finishing the provided subject and predicate on story paper. He underlines the subject with a yellow crayon and the predicate with a green crayon. Then he illustrates his work. Publish the projects in a class book titled "The Who's Who of [school's name] School."

Ruthie Titus
Poland, OH

Mr. Diaz and I are high-fiving.

Subject _____ and I
_____
(staff member)

Predicate
are _____.
(action)

Can of Worms

Subjects and predicates are the key to this can of worms! Begin with six sentences. Write the subject and predicate of each sentence on individual strips of tan paper. Then trim the strips into worm shapes. Store the cutouts in a clean can without sharp edges. Place the can of worms, a direction card, writing paper, crayons, and pencils at a center. A student combines the subjects and predicates to make six sentences that make sense. As she copies the sentences on her paper, she capitalizes and punctuates them. Then she underlines each subject and predicate as outlined on the direction card.

adapted from an idea by Susan Marie Stires
Sam Houston Elementary
Wichita Falls, TX

Can of Worms Directions
Arrange the worms to make six sentences that make sense.
Copy the sentences on your paper.
Add missing capital letters and punctuation.
Draw a brown line under each subject.
Draw a purple line under each predicate.

an earthworm   cannot see

the bird in the tree   is looking for a worm

earthworms   tunnel underground

Grammar & Sentence Skills

Capital Crimes

Crack the case of the **capitalization** blues with this center activity. Program each of several magnifying glass cutouts (patterns on page 46) with sentences that contain capitalization errors. Then store the cutouts and an answer key in an envelope labeled "Top Secret." Place the envelope, pencils, and a supply of paper at a center. A student removes a magnifying glass cutout from the envelope, reads the sentence, and then writes a corrected version of the sentence on his paper. He continues in this manner for each sentence. Then he uses the answer key to check his work.

Ann Barkhouse
Burton Ettinger School
Halifax, Nova Scotia, Canada

Pasta Punctuation

This **quotation mark** center will be the talk of the classroom! At a center stocked with paper, place a supply of sentence strips, a bowl of uncooked macaroni, permanent markers, and glue. For writing inspiration, cut out various magazine pictures of people. Glue the pictures onto construction paper and place them at the center. A student writes on her paper three sentences of dialogue inspired by one or more pictures, being sure to use quotation marks appropriately. Then she uses a marker to write a selected sentence on a sentence strip, gluing on macaroni noodles in place of the quotation marks.

Natalie Tanner
Houston, TX

Grammar & Sentence Skills

Nutty About Nouns!

In a nutshell—this **noun** center is loads of fun! Using the patterns on page 47, duplicate three nuts and three nut caps per student. Place the patterns at a center along with scissors, glue, a dictionary, and crayons or markers. A student cuts out three nuts and nut caps. He labels the caps "Person," "Place," and "Thing"; then he glues each cap to a nut. Next he programs each nut with five appropriate nouns. He refers to the dictionary for correct spellings and to confirm that the words he has chosen are nouns. When his noun lists are finished, he colors the leaves on each nut. After all students have completed the center, display the students' work on a bulletin board titled "Nutty About Nouns!"

Julie Decker
Abbotsford Elementary, Abbotsford, WI

Thing
1. car
2. bus
3. mouse
4. cow
5. fish

Place
1. school
2. ocean
3. store
4. barn
5. house

Person
1. baker
2. helper
3. cook
4. sheriff
5. teacher

Noun Hounds

When it comes to reviewing **common and proper nouns,** this partner game is "pawsitively" perfect! Copy page 48 to make a class supply plus one extra. Cut out the grid from one copy, and label each noun "C" or "P" to indicate whether it is a common or proper noun. Place the resulting answer key at a center along with the student copies, two small paper clips, pencils, and a supply of kidney beans.

One player uses a paper clip to spin. If he spins "common noun" or "proper noun," he finds a corresponding example on his gameboard and reads it aloud. He circles any letters that need to be capitalized and then places a bean on the space. If he spins "lost bone," he loses a turn. The second player takes a turn in the same manner. Alternate play continues, with players referring to the answer key as needed. The first player to mark five words in a row wins. Woof!

adapted from an idea by Brandi Nash
Andover, KS

Name Joe   **Noun Hounds**   Identifying Common and Proper Nouns

monday	july		danny	united states
horse	ben franklin	new york	pencil	october
kate	denver	state	florida
store			dog

common noun   lost bone

33

Grammar & Sentence Skills

Take a Spin!

Capitalization of **proper nouns** drives this geography-themed center! Place a map, a copy of the spinner on page 49, blank paper, a ruler, crayons, and pencils at a center. A student divides a sheet of paper into four columns and writes at the top of each column a different term from the provided spinner. Next, he spins the spinner. On the map he finds an example of the term that he spun, writes its name in the corresponding column of his paper, and underlines each capital letter. Then he spins the spinner again and repeats the procedure. Ask each child to record ten or more spins on his paper. Now that's a low-cost way to travel the country and practice capitalizing proper nouns!

Julie Ivory
Seton Catholic School
Davenport, IA

State	Capital City	Lake	River
Kentucky Oregon	Little Rock		Yukon River Snake River

Possessive Noun Pictures

Try this student-made center to help youngsters punctuate **possessive nouns**! To prepare, each child needs two 4" x 6" index cards. The child draws a line down the center of each one. He illustrates one half of a card with a person or animal. He illustrates the other half with a suitable possession. Then he labels his artwork with the appropriate nouns. He writes the corresponding possessive noun phrase on the back of his card, being sure to punctuate it correctly. He repeats this process to prepare his second card so that it shows plural possession. Collect the cards and check them for accuracy. Place the cards at a center with pencils and paper. A child selects a card, writes the corresponding possessive phrase, then flips the card to check his work.

Toni Rivard
Somerset Elementary
Somerset, WI

Grammar & Sentence Skills

Seasonal Nouns

Reinforce **plural and possessive nouns** with this flip-book project. Place crayons, scissors, pencils, and a supply of 9" x 12" drawing paper at a center. To make a flip book, a student folds a sheet of drawing paper in half (to 4½" x 12") and makes two equally spaced cuts in the top layer to create three flaps. She chooses a noun (a person or thing). On the first flap she illustrates the singular form of the noun; then she writes the singular noun under this flap. On the second flap she illustrates a plural form of the noun; then she writes the plural noun under this flap. On the third flap she illustrates the singular noun showing ownership; then, under this flap, she writes the singular possessive form of the noun. As an added challenge, ask each student to write (under each flap) a sentence that includes the featured noun form.

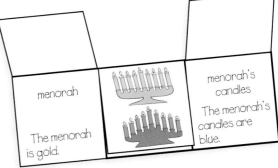

Tina E. Fox-Henderson
Christiansburg Primary School
Christiansburg, VA

Colorful Packs

Keep **singular and plural** skills sharp! Cut out three construction paper copies of the crayon patterns on page 50. Program each crayon with a listed word. Seal a letter-size envelope and then cut it in half. With the opening at the top, label one half "singular" and one half "plural." Color each half to resemble a crayon box. Cut out a copy of the answer key on page 51 and fold it in half. Place the crayons, boxes, and answer key at a center.

A student sorts the crayons into the appropriate boxes. Then she uses the key to check her work. Finally, she selects one crayon from each box and writes a sentence for each one. For a more challenging word sort, label crayon cutouts with singular words and a different box for each plural spelling pattern.

Singular Words	Plural Words
family	children
glass	feet
lunch	games
pencil	geese
rose	mice
shell	wolves

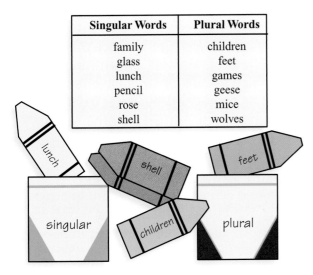

adapted from an idea by Mary Beth Godbout
Gilford, NH

Grammar & Sentence Skills

Snacktime Plurals

Plurals are food for thought at this tempting center. Cut out a copy of the potato chip bag and several copies of the potato chip patterns on page 52. For each plural rule shown, program several potato chip cutouts with singular nouns. Prepare an answer key with the corresponding plurals listed by rule. Place the potato chips, bag, answer key, and two small paper plates in a basket. Set the basket at a center stocked with paper and pencils. A student sorts the chips by rule onto the plates. For each group of words, she writes the corresponding plurals on her paper. She uses the key to check her work.

adapted from an idea by Robbye
    Spector—Special Education
Public School #29 Annex
Jersey City, NJ

Plural Chips

Add <u>s</u> to most nouns.
(chips)
Add <u>es</u> if the noun ends
in <u>ch</u>, <u>s</u>, <u>sh</u>, <u>x</u>, or <u>z</u>.
(lunches)

plate

bag   peach

Word List	
Singular	Plural
goose	geese
foot	feet
mouse	mice
die	dice
man	men
child	children
tooth	teeth
ox	oxen

teeth

J.C.

tooth

Tricky Plurals

Irregular plurals are in the cards! Copy and cut out the word list on page 51. Place the list at a center along with blank cards, crayons, and pencils. A student initials five blank cards. On one side of each card he copies and illustrates a different singular noun from the list. On the other side of each card he copies and illustrates the plural form of the noun. Store the cards at the center.

For a follow-up activity, remove the list of plurals from the center. A twosome shuffles and stacks the cards. Partner 1 reads aloud the top card. If the word is singular, he provides the plural form of the word, and vice versa. Partner 2 flips the card to verify the answer. Then the card is placed on the bottom of the stack. Play alternates between the partners for as long as desired.

Sue Miller
Helen H. Hansen Elementary
Stoughton, MA

Grammar & Sentence Skills

Pick a Pronoun

Provide plenty of **pronoun practice** at this easy-to-prepare center. Label one container for each pronoun you wish to spotlight. Next, program individual cards with corresponding nouns. Laminate the cards and then use a permanent marker to code the backs for self-checking. Store the cards in a gift bag. Place the gift bag and the labeled containers at a center. A student sorts the cards and then flips them to check her work.

Janet Bavonese
James H. Bright Elementary
Miami, FL

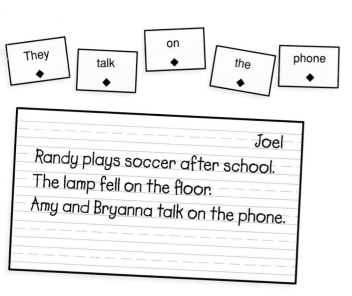

Pronoun Replacements

Students link **pronouns** to nouns at this sentence-building center. Cut out a construction paper copy of the cards from page 53. Store them at a center along with writing paper, crayons, and pencils. A student sorts the cards by symbols, and then he arranges the cards in each set to make a complete sentence. When he writes each sentence on his paper, he replaces each pronoun with an appropriate noun or nouns.

adapted from an idea by Cynthia Holcomb
Irion County Elementary
Mertzon, TX

Grammar & Sentence Skills

Action Pack

This center is packed with opportunities for using **action verbs!** Stuff a backpack with props that suggest action, such as a jump rope, ball, spoon, ruler, book, and drinking cup. Place the backpack, half sheets of blank paper, crayons, and pencils at the center. A student selects a prop from the backpack and brainstorms actions associated with it. Then, on each side of a half sheet of paper, she writes and illustrates a different action sentence about the prop and uses a crayon to underline each action word she uses. When every child has completed the center, compile the students' work into a class booklet titled "Ready for Action!"

adapted from an idea by
Linda Masternak Justice
Kansas City, MO

Diane throws the ball as far as she can.

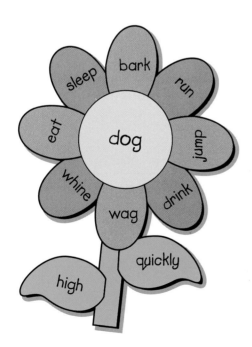

Verb Garden

Sprout a review of **verbs!** Place construction paper, green paper stems, markers or crayons, scissors, and glue at a center along with templates for petals and leaves (see page 54) and a seven-inch circle. Using the templates, a child traces one circle, two leaf shapes, and several petal shapes on construction paper. She cuts along the resulting outlines and then she uses the cutouts, a paper stem, and glue to make a flower. When the glue is dry, she writes a noun in the flower center. On each petal she writes a different action verb the noun can do. (Challenge older students to also label each leaf with an adverb that modifies a featured verb.) Post the students' work at the center. The following week have students use the resulting verb garden as inspiration for a writing activity.

Julie Decker
Abbotsford Elementary
Abbotsford, WI

Grammar & Sentence Skills

Verbs Are Vital!

Get to the heart of **verbs** at this kid-pleasing center. Place two heart-shaped templates (one slightly larger than the other), story paper, red or pink construction paper, pencils, scissors, glue, and crayons at a center. A student traces the smaller template on a sheet of story paper and cuts out the resulting shape. He writes a complete sentence on the heart-shaped paper, uses a red or pink crayon to underline each verb he used, and illustrates his sentence. Next he traces the larger template on red (or pink) paper, cuts out the resulting shape, and mounts his written work atop the colorful heart cutout. Display these completed projects on a bulletin board titled "Verbs Are Vital—Sentences Can't Live Without Them!"

Cynthia Adams
Jefferson Elementary
Hobbs, NM

My dog barks a lot.

"Sense-ational" Adjectives

Take a five-senses approach to **adjectives!** Display a cotton ball, a marble, and a piece of sandpaper at a center, and provide crayons, pencils, and blank paper. A student visually divides a sheet of paper into fourths and uses a crayon to title one box for each of the three objects on display. In the fourth box he names a favorite snack food. Below each noun he lists three to five adjectives that describe how the object looks, sounds, feels, smells, or might taste. (Caution students not to taste any of the objects.) Then, on the back of his paper, he writes and illustrates a descriptive sentence about one or more of the objects.

Josephine Flammer
Brook Avenue School
Bay Shore, NY

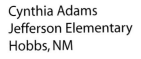

cotton ball	marble
fluffy soft white small	smooth round red hard small
sandpaper	popcorn
thin bumpy rough scratchy brown	salty yummy small fresh crunchy

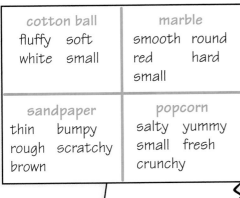

The smooth, red marble rolled into my bag of small, crunchy popcorn.

39

Grammar & Sentence Skills

Silly Sentences

Reviewing **parts of speech** can lead to giggles and chuckles at this center! To make a silly-sentence booklet for each student, fold five sheets of blank paper into fourths as shown; then unfold the papers and staple them between two construction-paper covers. Place the booklets, pencils, crayons, and scissors at a center. A student personalizes the cover of a booklet. Then, starting at the top of each blank page, he writes a four-word sentence—one word per section—in the following order: an adjective, a plural noun, a present-tense action verb, an adverb. When all five pages have been programmed, he cuts each page into fourths. To do this he starts at the right margin of every page and cuts along each fold line until he is about one inch from the left margin. To read his booklet, the student randomly flips the strips and reads the resulting four-word sentences from top to bottom.

Cindy Marks
Mark Twain Elementary School
Kirkland, WA

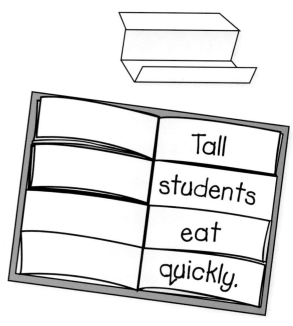

"Hearts" of Speech

Students will take this **parts-of-speech** center to heart! Cut out several construction paper copies of the heart cookies on page 55. Label each heart with a different message. Underline a part of speech on each heart and program the back of the cutout with the corresponding part-of-speech name. Label one cookie tin for each part of speech being reviewed. Place the labeled cookie tins and a cookie sheet at a center. Arrange the heart cutouts on the cookie sheet. A student sorts the cookies into the tins; then he removes the cookies from each tin to check his work.

Heather Graley
Eaton, OH

1. Cut out three verbs. Use each verb in a different sentence.

2. Cut out a noun and an adjective. Use the two words in a sentence.

3. Cut out two adjectives. Use the two words in a sentence.

4. Cut out a noun, an adjective, and a verb. Use the three words in a sentence.

5. Cut out a noun and a verb. Use the two words in a sentence.

6. Cut out two nouns. Use the two words in a sentence.

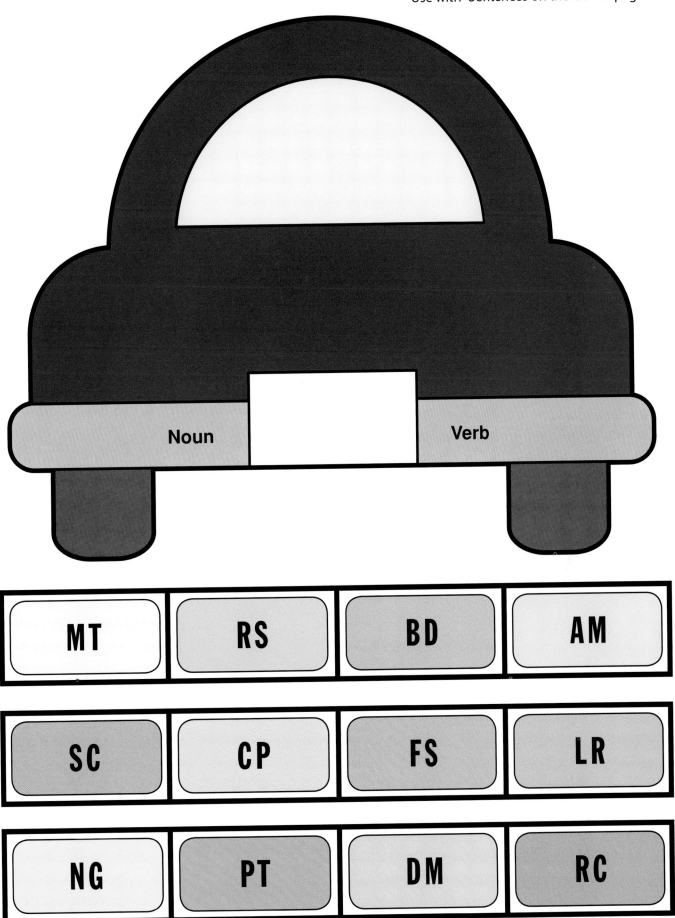

Noun

Verb

MT	RS	BD	AM
SC	CP	FS	LR
NG	PT	DM	RC

TEC61024

TEC61024   TEC61024   TEC61024   TEC61024

TEC61024   TEC61024   TEC61024   TEC61024

TEC61024   TEC61024   TEC61024   TEC61024

44

TEC61024

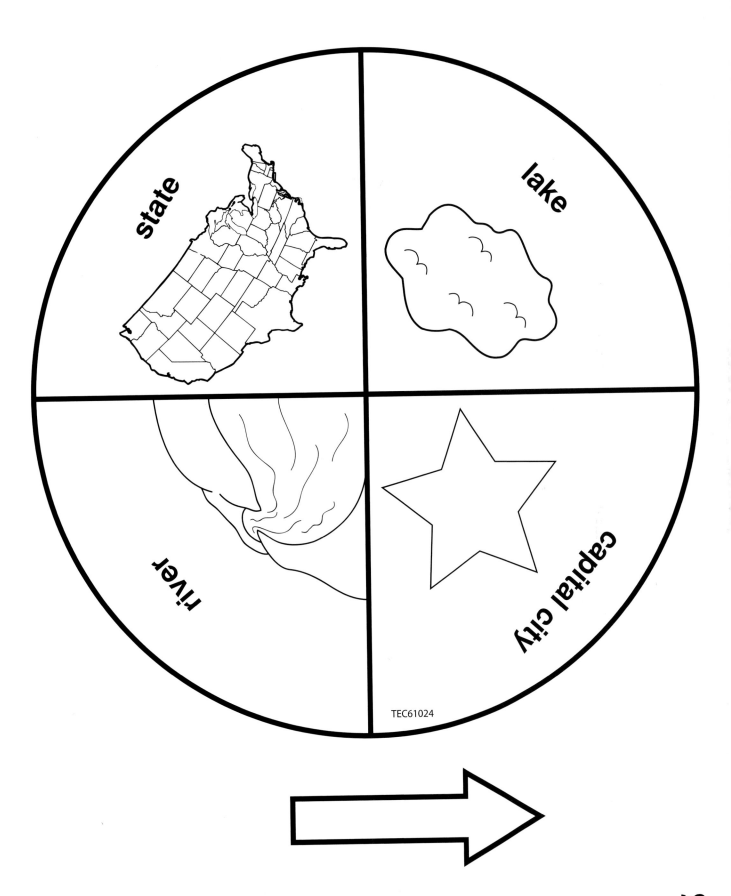

state

lake

river

capital city

Crayon Patterns

Use with "Colorful Packs" on page 35.

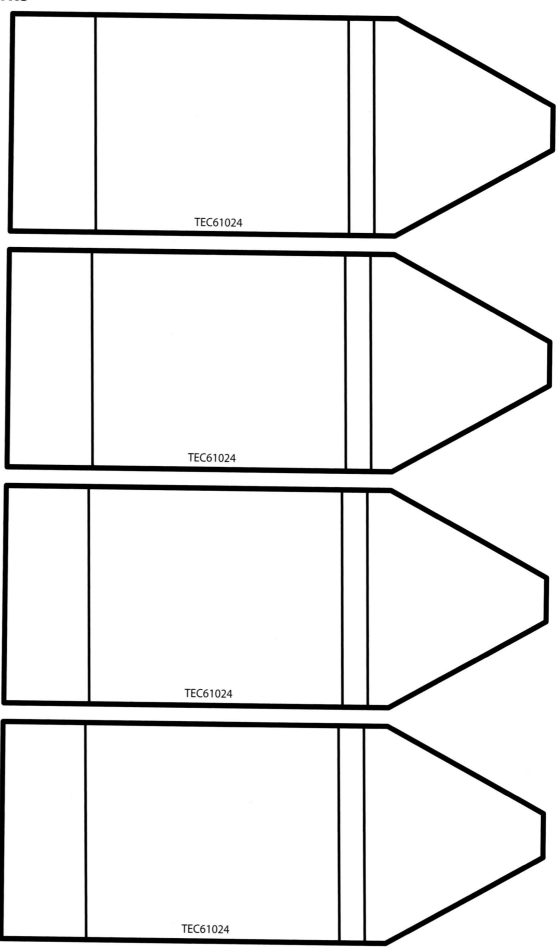

TEC61024

TEC61024

TEC61024

TEC61024

Singular Words	Plural Words
family	children
glass	feet
lunch	games
pencil	geese
rose	mice
shell	wolves

TEC61024

Word List

Plural	Singular
geese	goose
feet	foot
mice	mouse
dice	die
men	man
children	child
teeth	tooth
oxen	ox

TEC61024

Potato Chip Bag and Chip Patterns

Use with "Snacktime Plurals" on page 36.

Plural Chips

- Add **s** to most nouns. (chips)

- Add **es** if the noun ends in **ch**, **s**, **sh**, **x**, or **z**. (lunches)

TEC61024

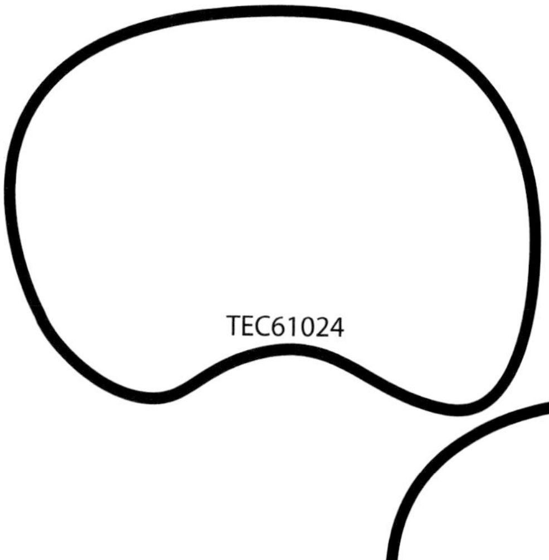

TEC61024

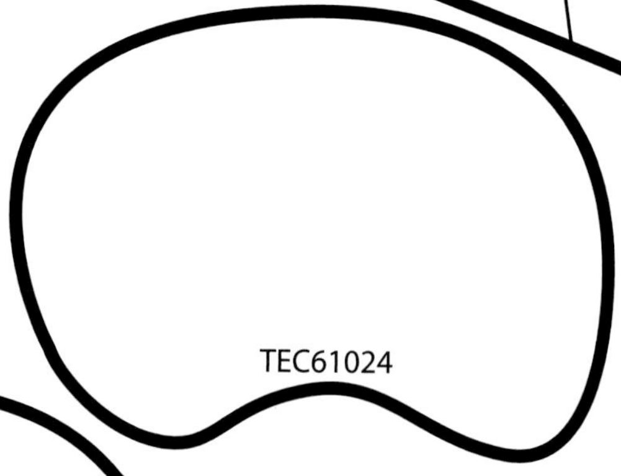

TEC61024

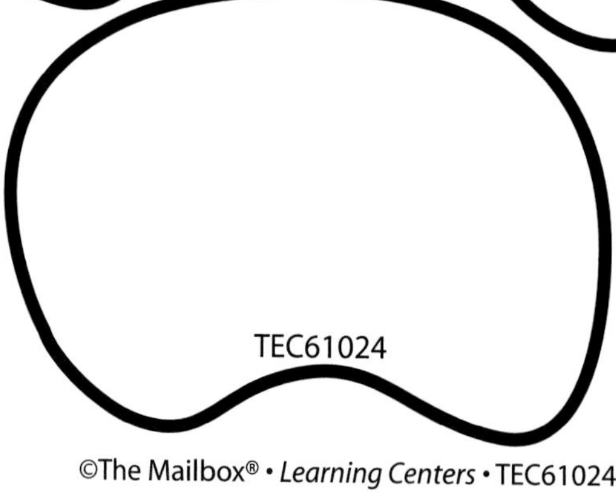

TEC61024

She ■ TEC61024	waved ■ TEC61024	at ■ TEC61024	the ■ TEC61024	principal. ■ TEC61024
He ● TEC61024	plays ● TEC61024	soccer ● TEC61024	after ● TEC61024	school. ● TEC61024
It ▲ TEC61024	fell ▲ TEC61024	on ▲ TEC61024	the ▲ TEC61024	floor. ▲ TEC61024
They ◆ TEC61024	talk ◆ TEC61024	on ◆ TEC61024	the ◆ TEC61024	phone. ◆ TEC61024
We ⬮ TEC61024	like ⬮ TEC61024	to ⬮ TEC61024	play ⬮ TEC61024	together. ⬮ TEC61024

Petal and Leaf Patterns
Use with "Verb Garden" on page 38.

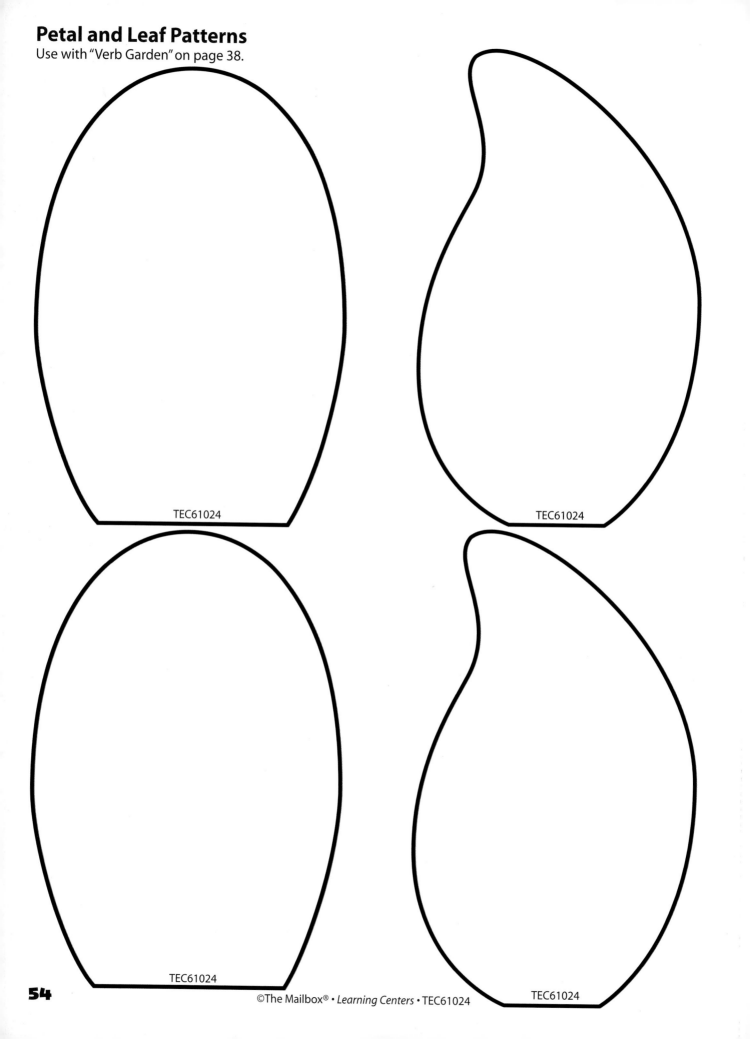

TEC61024

TEC61024

TEC61024

TEC61024

Teapot Travels

This **creative-writing** center is the ticket to adventure! Place a teapot, story paper, pencils, and crayons at the center. Each week select a different travel destination and display resources at the center that describe and picture this place. A student gently rubs the teapot and pretends he is magically transported to the featured destination. Using the provided resources, he imagines himself having an adventure there. He rubs the teapot a second time for his return trip. Then he writes and illustrates a story about his adventure.

Theresa DeShong
Nut Swamp School
Middletown, NJ

The Grand Canyon

My trip to the Grand Canyon was exciting! I rode a mule to the very bottom of the canyon. There is a big river there. I saw some people floating on a raft. My mule sure got tired carrying me back to the top of the canyon. I got a little scared, but we made it!

Writing Treasure

There's a booty of **creative-writing** inspiration at this center! Decorate a box (with a removable lid) so that it resembles a treasure chest. Place the chest, story paper, pencils, crayons, and a student dictionary at a center. Each week stock the chest with four or five items that will encourage creative writing. A student removes the items from the chest, and then he writes and illustrates a story that is inspired by them. If desired, compile each week's stories into a class book titled "Weekly Writing Treasures From [date]."

Ruthie Jamieson Titus
Union Elementary
Poland, OH

The Magic Biscuit

Once upon a time a dog ate a very yummy biscuit. It was...

"Tree-mendous" Writing!

Students won't want to "leaf" this **creative-writing** center! Display a paper tree trunk at a center. Next number and program each of several fall-colored leaf cutouts with different story starters. Also number a writing journal to correspond with each leaf. Pin the leaves on the tree, and place the journals and several pencils at the center. A student selects a leaf, then copies the story starter and writes his story in the corresponding journal. When he is finished writing, he signs his name, closes the journal, and returns the leaf to the tree. One student may visit the center several times—choosing a different story starter each visit. Keep writing interest high by routinely replacing the story starters and their corresponding journals.

Kathleen Lynch
St. Aloysius School
Jackson, NJ

4. One day when I was raking leaves,...

#5 #6

Billy

One day when I was raking leaves, I noticed a bright purple leaf in my pile. I picked it up and it said, "Hello!" I could hardly believe my ears! The leaf said his name was Leonard but that I could call him Leo. He said he had magical powers. I wasn't sure

Invent a Pet!

Unleash your youngsters' creativity at this one-of-a-kind **writing** center! Enlist your students' help in creating a list of pets. Place the resulting list at a center, along with a supply of story paper, pencils, and crayons or markers. A student invents a new kind of pet by combining two pet names. She writes the name of her unique pet on a sheet of paper; then she illustrates the pet and writes about its unique abilities. Compile the pet-related projects in a class book for further reading enjoyment!

Laura Horowitz
Embassy Creek Elementary
Cooper City, FL

Pet List

kitten   ferret
puppy   canary
iguana   parakeet
horse   tarantula
rabbit   parrot
snake   llama
goldfish   guinea pig
turtle   hermit crab
hamster
gerbil
lizard

Parabit
A parabit is very cool because it hops around like a rabbit and it sings like a parakeet. It can fly too. A parabit is also very smart. It can learn tricks.

Shoe Swap

This **writing** center is a real "shoe-in"! Gather several pairs of high-interest adult-size shoes, such as cowboy boots, ballet slippers, high-heeled shoes, snowshoes, fishing boots, ski boots, army boots, tap shoes, and high-top sneakers. Place the shoes, a supply of story paper, and crayons or markers at a center. A student slips her stocking feet into a pair of shoes and imagines her life as an adult in these shoes. Then she writes and illustrates a story about one of her adventures.

Krista K. Zimmerman
Tuckerton Elementary School
Tuckerton, NJ

The Big One
I had a bite. Boy, did I have a bite! My fishing pole was jumping all over the place. I lost my lucky fishing cap; then I lost my fish! But I didn't give up! And the next time...

"Look how strong I am!" Mr. Jack bragged.

Mrs. Cohen exclaimed, "You're dripping water all over the floor!"

Mrs. Cohen and Mr. Jack

Say What?

This **dialogue-writing** center gives students something to talk about! Take and develop several humorous photographs of pairs of faculty members. Mount each photograph at the bottom of a vertically positioned 9" x 12" sheet of construction paper. Label each photograph with the faculty members' names, and staple several half sheets of writing paper to the top of each sheet. Place the resulting writing prompts at a center. On a blank page of a selected prompt, a child writes a brief conversation inspired by the photograph. Then she checks her use of quotation marks and other punctuation.

When a prompt has no more blank pages, place it in a three-ring binder designated for this purpose. Encourage students to use the compiled conversations for rib-tickling reading practice!

Ruthie Jamieson Titus
Union Elementary
Poland, OH

Writing

"Apple-icious" Acrostics

Get to the core of **descriptive writing!** Make a red construction paper copy of the apple patterns on page 64. Also cut a supply of 6" x 9" rectangles of white paper. Place the precut paper, the apple patterns, scraps of green paper and brown paper, scissors, glue, a black crayon, and pencils at a center. A student uses the black crayon to write her name vertically down the left margin of a white paper rectangle. Then she writes a self-describing word or phrase that begins with each letter of her name. To make the apple project pictured, she trims around her resulting acrostic poem. Next, she cuts out her apple patterns and glues her acrostic poem between the two cutouts. Then she fashions a stem and leaf from scrap paper, and glues the cutouts in place. Now that's an "a-peel-ing" writing project!

Jane Manuel
Wellington, TX

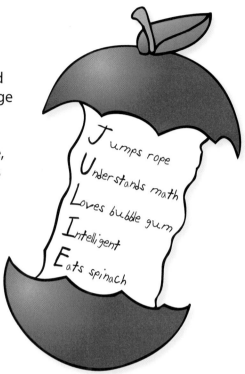

Jumps rope
Understands math
Loves bubble gum
Intelligent
Eats spinach

What's the Scoop?

At this **writing** center students write just-for-fun newspaper articles. Use a blue marker to label an envelope "Who?" and to write the names of several different people on individual paper strips. Place the color-coded strips in the envelope. In a similar manner create a color-coded envelope and a set of paper strips for each of the following questions: What?, When?, Where?, Why?, How? Store the envelopes, writing paper, and pencils at a center. A student selects a paper strip from each envelope and incorporates the information into a newsy story. After each student has completed the center, edit the stories and have each youngster write his final draft on a five-inch-wide strip of writing paper. Glue the students' work onto the pages of a discarded newspaper; then place this hot-off-the-press edition in your classroom library for all to read.

Mary Anne Murphy
Andrew Jackson Language Academy
Chicago, IL

Who?
the school principal

What?
saw a spaceship

When?
at midnight

Where?
at the beach

How?

Why?

At about midnight last night, Mr. Adams spotted a spaceship. He was

Lots of Lists!

Reinforce selected skills or topics with this versatile **list-making** idea. On each of several blank cards, identify a different list for students to write, specifying the number of words or items. Place the cards in a labeled container. Set the container at a center stocked with a stapler, 4½" x 12" construction paper strips, and writing paper that has been cut in half lengthwise. A student randomly takes a card and appropriately titles a piece of writing paper. He writes a numbered list and then returns the card to the container. As time allows, he makes additional lists in the same manner. He stacks his completed lists on a construction paper strip and staples the entire stack at the top.

Valerie Wood Smith
Morgantown, PA

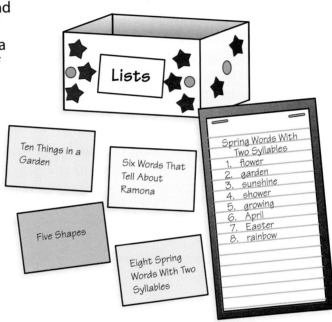

Lists

Ten Things in a Garden

Six Words That Tell About Ramona

Five Shapes

Eight Spring Words With Two Syllables

Spring Words With Two Syllables
1. flower
2. garden
3. sunshine
4. shower
5. growing
6. April
7. Easter
8. rainbow

Top Ten Favorites

Here's a center that's sure to make your students' top ten **list** of **writing** activities! On each of several cards, write a different category, such as games, foods, books, and outdoor activities. Place the cards at a center along with pencils and a supply of writing paper. A student chooses a category card, titles his paper "[Student's name]'s Top Ten [category]," and lists his ten favorites for that category. Invite students to write top ten lists for as many categories as time allows. Later, sort the lists by categories and compile each collection into a class book for your youngsters' reading enjoyment.

places to visit

foods

ways to make friends

animals

Ben's Top Ten Places to Visit
1. Waterland Wave Park
2. Grandma's house
3. the park near my house
4. the museum
5. the beach
6. Tommy's house
7. the state fair
8. the zoo
9. the library
10. the toy store

Mail Matters

Here's a center that delivers improved **letter-writing skills!** Label a large, empty tissue box "Mail" and remove the plastic from the box opening. Place the resulting mailbox at a center along with a list of suggested in-school mail recipients. Stock the center with letter-writing supplies, such as pencils, stationery, index cards (postcards), and small envelopes or stickers to seal folded letters. Add student references, such as a list of possible letter-writing topics or letter-formatting guidelines.

To use the center, a youngster writes a letter to a chosen student or staff member. She uses established guidelines to edit her writing. She prepares the letter for hand delivery and then drops it in the mailbox for designated student mail carriers to collect.

adapted from an idea by Janet Robbins
Fairview Elementary School
Richmond, IN

Mail

Mr. Jakes
Cafeteria
Fairview Elementary School

Special Delivery

Deliver year-round **letter-writing** practice at this versatile center. Write your students' names on individual slips of paper; then deposit the papers in a decorated container. Place the container, a supply of lined paper or stationery, an assortment of writing instruments, and a letter receptacle at a center. Also display a colorful poster that shows the parts of a friendly letter. To complete the center, a student draws the name of a classmate from the container and writes a letter to the classmate. Then he places his completed letter in the letter receptacle and discards the paper slip. When each child has visited the center—and the container of student names is empty—ask a student or two to deliver the student-written letters. On his second center visit, a student writes a letter to the classmate who wrote to him. Once these letters have been delivered, restock the decorated container with student names and begin the letter-writing process again.

Mauri A. Capps
Northlake Elementary
Dallas, TX

David Young

Oct. 20, 2007

Dear David,
I was so excited to draw your name! I think you are the best. I loved the joke you told

Wanted: Perfect Summer

Put your youngsters' **writing** skills to the test when you ask them to pen classified ads for the perfect summer! Read aloud several classified ads and discuss with students the kinds of information included in the ads. If desired, also read aloud your local paper's guidelines for writing these ads. Place several samples of classified ads, a supply of writing paper, and pencils at a center. A student writes a brief ad seeking the perfect summer. After each student has completed the center and the ads have been edited, have each student copy his ad on a two-inch-wide paper strip. Mount the ads on blank paper to resemble pages from the "classifieds"; then duplicate a class supply for students to read over the summer. Extra! Extra! Read all about it!

adapted from an idea by Tammy Brinkman and
    Kimberly Martin
San Antonio, TX

Wanted: Perfect Summer

All day cartoons, daily trip to the playground, hot dog or hamburger lunch, ice cream daily at 3:00, 2 hours of swimming, weekly trips to the movies. Call 123-4567.

Strawberry Wishes

At this center, students **write for a purpose.** Place copies of the poem from page 65 at a center along with 9" x 12" sheets of light-colored construction paper, half sheets of writing paper, a red stamp pad, crayons, glue, scissors, and pencils. A student folds a sheet of construction paper in half (to 6" x 9"), cuts out a copy of the poem, glues the poem to the front of the card, and adds a desired greeting. Then she writes on a half sheet of writing paper three or more wishes for the intended recipient of her card. She glues her writing inside the card, adds a closing, and signs her name. To embellish her work with strawberries, she uses the ink pad to make red thumbprints on the card and then adds details to the prints as shown. Very sweet!

Amy Climer
Houston Elementary
Cincinnati, OH

I wish you never had to wash dishes again!
I wish Aunt Laura lived closer!
I wish you could meet Ricky Martin!
I wish you got to stay home every day!
Happy Mother's Day!
I love you!
XOOXX,
Olivia

Dear Mom,
Sweet Wishes for You!
My wishes for you are so sweet.
I hope they knock you off your feet!
I wrote them carefully by hand
Because I am your biggest fan!

Apple Pattern
Use with "'Apple-icious' Acrostics" on page 60.

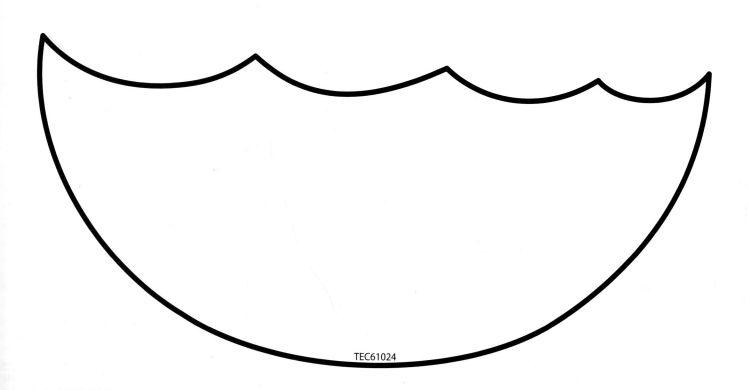

TEC61024

Sweet Wishes for You!

My wishes for you are so sweet.
I hope they knock you off your feet!
I wrote them carefully by hand
Because I am your biggest fan!

©The Mailbox® • *Learning Centers* • TEC61024

Sweet Wishes for You!

My wishes for you are so sweet.
I hope they knock you off your feet!
I wrote them carefully by hand
Because I am your biggest fan!

©The Mailbox® • *Learning Centers* • TEC61024

Sweet Wishes for You!

My wishes for you are so sweet.
I hope they knock you off your feet!
I wrote them carefully by hand
Because I am your biggest fan!

©The Mailbox® • *Learning Centers* • TEC61024

Reading Comprehension

Main Idea Match

Serve up practice with **main idea and supporting details.** Select three short reading passages for this purpose. For each selection, copy and cut out the cookie jar pattern from page 69. Then label each with the main idea, and program three or four construction paper cookies with supporting details. Number the jars. Then code the back of each cookie with the number of the corresponding jar. Store the cookies in a nonbreakable cookie tin. Place the tin and jars at a center. A student reads the jars and cookies. Then she sorts the cookies onto the appropriate jars. She flips the cookies to check her work.

adapted from an idea by Virginia Zeletzki
Banyan Creek Elementary School
Delray Beach, FL

Comic Capers

This **sequencing** activity will have students grinning from ear to ear. From discarded newspapers, cut several comic strips that are appropriate for your students. For each comic strip, cut apart the individual frames and mount each frame on a construction paper rectangle. Number the backs of the rectangles to show the correct order of the strip. Store each set of rectangles in a numbered envelope. Store the envelopes at a center along with crayons or markers, pencils, and 4" x 18" strips of paper. A student sequences the rectangles from each envelope and checks her work. Then she uses the provided supplies to draw and color a comic strip of her own!

Tammy Brinkman & Kimberly Martin
Dellview Elementary
San Antonio, TX

Picturing Facts and Opinions

Students report **facts and opinions** at this picture-perfect activity. Place scissors, a ruler, glue, pencils, discarded catalogs and magazines, and a supply of drawing paper at a center. A student cuts out a desired picture and glues it near the top of her paper. Below the picture, she draws two columns and labels one "Facts" and the other "Opinions." Next, she studies the picture and lists five facts and five opinions about it. If desired, ask each child to confirm with a classmate that her facts are facts and her opinions are opinions before she submits her work. The end result is a much clearer understanding of fact and opinion!

Joyce Hovanec
Glassport Elementary
Glassport, PA

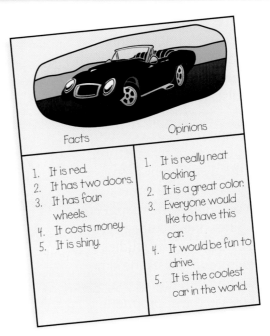

Facts	Opinions
1. It is red.	1. It is really neat looking.
2. It has two doors.	2. It is a great color.
3. It has four wheels.	3. Everyone would like to have this car.
4. It costs money.	4. It would be fun to drive.
5. It is shiny.	5. It is the coolest car in the world.

Whales

Facts	Opinions
Whales are mammals.	Whales are scary.
Whales are warm-blooded.	Dolphins are more fun to watch than whales.
Blue whales are the biggest animals.	Blue whales are awesome.

Is That a Fact?

Highlight **facts and opinions** at this center. At a center, place paper, pencils, and several objects or pictures that represent content-area topics your students have studied. A student selects an item and draws a two-column chart on her paper. She titles the chart with the appropriate topic. She labels one column "Facts" and the other column "Opinions." She recalls what she learned about the topic and lists three or more statements in each column.

Laura Wagner
Raleigh, NC

Reading Comprehension

Same and Different

This easy-to-make center provides plenty of practice with **comparing and contrasting!** Place discarded catalogs, scissors, glue, pencils, and a supply of drawing paper at a center. A student cuts out two pictures of distinctly different items from a catalog. She draws a Venn diagram on her paper and then glues one picture above each circle. Next she studies the pictures and lists the similarities and differences that she observes in the appropriate areas of the diagram.

Kimberly Minafo
Dillard Drive Elementary
Raleigh, NC

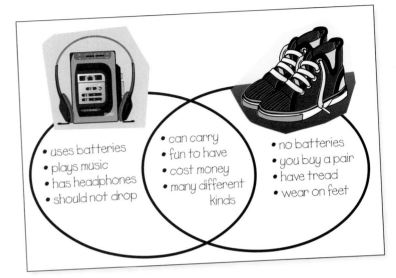

- uses batteries
- plays music
- has headphones
- should not drop

- can carry
- fun to have
- cost money
- many different kinds

- no batteries
- you buy a pair
- have tread
- wear on feet

Playtime!

Simple toys are the only items needed in this **cause-and-effect** center. Enlist your youngsters' help in gathering several toys that represent cause-and-effect relationships, such as a pull toy that makes noise, a jack-in-the-box, and any type of windup toy. Place the toys at a center along with a supply of paper. A student visits the center and plays with each of five different toys. On his paper, he describes each toy in a cause-and-effect sentence. Collect the students' papers. Later, when all students have completed the center, return the students' papers and, as a class, discuss the youngsters' sentences and observations.

Reference Skills

The White Pages

A discarded phone book makes a perfect **alphabetizing** center! Place the phone book, a supply of paper, and pencils at a center. Post a task card listing a series of business phone numbers that you would like your students to look up. On their papers, have the youngsters record the name of each business, its phone number, and the page of the phone book where the number was found. Provide an answer key if desired. Display a different task card each week and let the students' fingers do the alphabetizing!

Rebekah Howell
Taylors Creek Elementary
Hinesville, GA

Letter-Perfect Lists

Line up practice with **ABC order.** Program a supply of seasonal cutouts with words appropriate for your students' alphabetizing skills. Place the cutouts in a gift bag and label the bag with the number of words that you would like students to alphabetize at one time. Place the bag at a center stocked with paper. A student takes the designated number of cutouts at random. He arranges the cutouts in ABC order and then lists the sequenced words on his paper. He returns the cutouts to the bag and scrambles them. Then he takes another selection of cutouts from the bag and uses them to write a second list.

adapted from an idea by Jen Ratka
Hillview Elementary School
Lancaster, NY

Guide Word Sort

Create an appetite for **guide words?** You bet! Cut a supply of ¾" x 4" yellow paper strips (for french fries). Also cut out and assemble the fry boxes on page 73. Laminate the pieces; then use an X-acto knife to reopen the pocket of each holder. Next, with a permanent marker, write a different guide word pair on each holder. Program the french fries with corresponding entry words. For self-checking, mark the back of each holder and its corresponding fries with the same symbol. A student sorts the french fries into the holders; then she flips each holder to check her work!

Martha Kelly
Roanoke, VA

"Soup-er" Guide Words

Stir up extra **guide word practice!** First, copy and cut out the answer key on page 75. Next, label each of five plastic bowls with a different guide word pair (from the key) and program individual craft sticks with the entry words provided. Store the sticks in a container decorated to resemble a soup can. Place the container, the plastic bowls, and the answer key at a center. A student sorts the craft sticks into the appropriate bowls. Then he uses the answer key to check his work.

Erin Harp
Manchester, NH

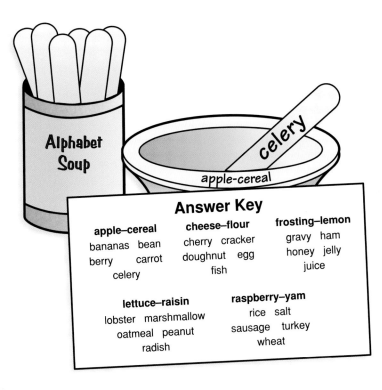

Answer Key

apple–cereal
bananas bean
berry   carrot
      celery

cheese–flour
cherry cracker
doughnut egg
      fish

frosting–lemon
gravy ham
honey jelly
      juice

lettuce–raisin
lobster marshmallow
oatmeal peanut
      radish

raspberry–yam
rice salt
sausage turkey
      wheat

Reference Skills

Guide Words Galore

Guide word practice becomes a real "shoe-in" at this sorting center. Suspend a plastic shoe organizer at a center. Number and label each pocket with a different pair of guide words. Make sure the guide word pairs do not alphabetically overlap. For each pocket, copy, cut out, and label one shoeprint pattern from page 75 with an appropriate entry word. Program the back of the cutout with the matching pocket number. Laminate the shoeprint cutouts for durability, if desired; then store them in a shoebox at the center. A student sorts the cutouts into the shoe organizer. When all the shoeprints have been sorted, he turns each one over to check his work.

Margaret-Ann Rhem
Western Branch Intermediate
Chesapeake, VA

Dig In!

Students dig into the **dictionary** at this center! Choose from a student dictionary a class supply of words that may be unfamiliar to your youngsters. Write each word at the top of a sheet of construction paper and store the labeled sheets in a folder. Place the folder, a student dictionary, crayons, a hole puncher, a binder, a supply of paper, and instructions at a center. A student chooses a sheet from the folder and follows the instructions. When her work is done, she hole-punches her project and places it in the binder in alphabetical order. The binder becomes a one-of-a-kind dictionary with plenty of kid appeal!

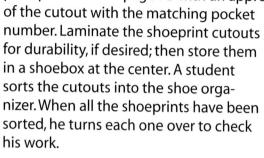

Dig In!

1. Find the word in the dictionary.
2. Illustrate the word.
3. In your own words, write what this word means.
4. Write your name on the back of the paper.

lynx

no tail

It is a wild cat that doesn't have a tail. It has thick fur. Its ears are even furry!

TEC61024

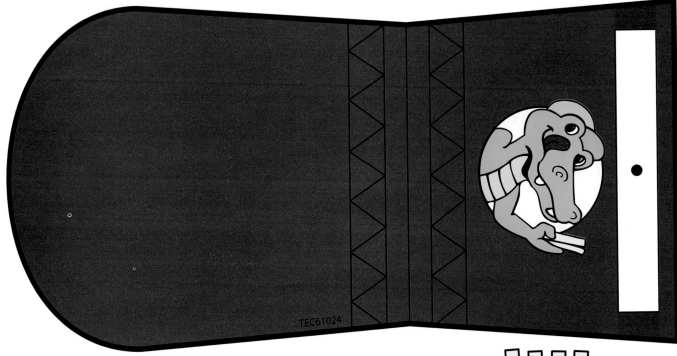

TEC61024

Fold.

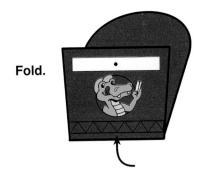

GLUE

Glue.

Finished Sample

73

Answer Key

apple–cereal
bananas   bean
berry   carrot
celery

cheese–flour
cherry   cracker
doughnut   egg
fish

frosting–lemon
gravy   ham
honey   jelly
juice

lettuce–raisin
lobster   marshmallow
oatmeal   peanut
radish

raspberry–yam
rice   salt
sausage   turkey
wheat

TEC61024

Shoe Pattern
Use with "Guide Words Galore" on page 72.

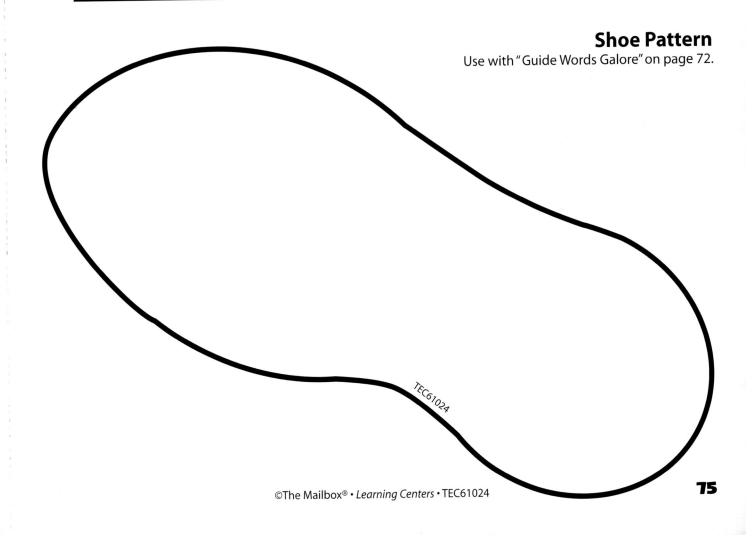

TEC61024

Number & Operations

Odd or Even?

Reinforce the concepts of **odd and even** at this easy-to-create center. Store blank paper, pencils, a pair of dice, and a supply of colorful peel-and-stick dots at a center. A student divides a sheet of blank paper into two columns and labels one column "Odd" and the other column "Even." Next the youngster rolls the dice and determines if the number he rolled is odd or even. He then creates and labels a matching dot set in the appropriate column of his paper. He continues in this manner until he has three or more different dot sets in each column.

Kim Wong
Olney Elementary School
Olney, MD

All Smiles

Your youngsters will be all smiles as they complete this **ordinal number word** center. For each student, label a long, narrow paper strip with a series of ten happy faces. (Older students may draw their own.) Copy and cut out the word bank on page 99. Program a set of directions for the students to follow. Laminate the word bank and directions for durability; then place the paper strips, word bank, and directions at a center along with pencils and crayons or markers. A student writes the corresponding ordinal number word above each happy face on his paper strip; then he carefully reads and follows the directions.

Gina Parisi
Demarest Elementary School
Bloomfield, NJ

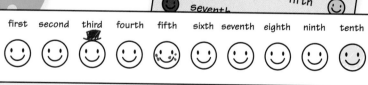

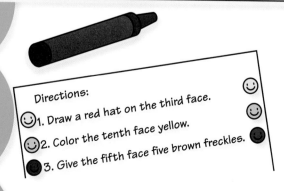

Skip-Counting Stones

Skip-counting practice is just a stone's throw away! Use a marker to label a gray construction paper stone for each number in a desired skip-counting sequence. Arrange the stones in order and then letter the backs of them for self-checking. Place the stones in a resealable plastic bag. Program additional sets of stones with various skip-counting sequences, using a different color of marker for each set. Place the bags at a center. A student selects a bag, removes the stones, and then sequences them. She flips the stones to check her work. What a rock-solid review of number patterns!

Michelle Sommerfeldt
Spitler Elementary
Hart, MI

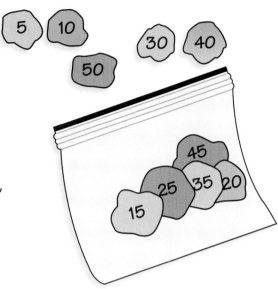

All in Order

Put a spin on **ordering three-digit numbers!** Prepare a paper clip spinner labeled as shown. Program six blank cards with three-digit numbers and then place them in a resealable plastic bag. Use different numbers to prepare a desired number of additional card sets. (For easy management, use cards of a different color for each set.) Set the bags, the spinner, and a paper clip at a center stocked with paper and pencils.

A student draws a line across the middle of a vertically positioned sheet of paper. He labels each half with a phrase from the spinner. Next, he spins the spinner. He sequences a chosen set of cards as indicated, writes the numbers in order in the appropriate section of his paper, and then returns the cards. He repeats the process with additional card sets as time allows.

Linnae Nicholas
Rushford Elementary School
Rushford, NY

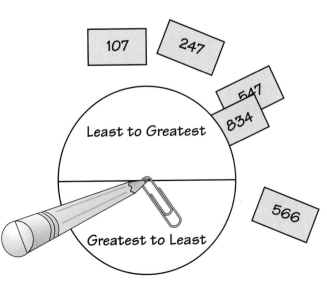

Roll 100!

Strengthen **place value and addition** skills with a partner game! Place a die, paper, and pencils at a center. To begin, each player rolls the die and writes the number she rolls on her paper as a one or a ten. (For example, if a child rolls a three, she may record the roll as 3 or 30.) Then each player rolls the die again, records her number (as a one or ten), and adds it to her previous roll. Play continues in this manner until each child tallies seven rolls. The winner of the game is the player whose total score is closer to, but not over, 100. Roll on!

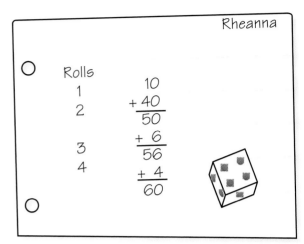

Jacki Itchkow
Public School 165 Q
Flushing, NY

Tens Tools

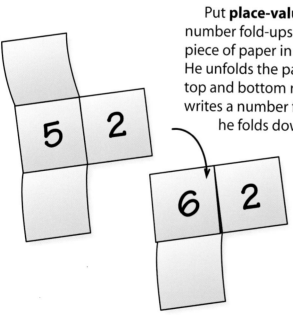

Put **place-value** practice at students' fingertips! To prepare number fold-ups for center use, each student folds a 6" x 9" piece of paper in half lengthwise and then in thirds (to 3" x 3"). He unfolds the paper, positions it vertically, and cuts away the top and bottom right-hand sections. In each middle section, he writes a number from 1 to 8 to form a two-digit number. Next, he folds down the top flap and writes the number that is one more than the concealed digit. He unfolds the paper, folds up the bottom flap, and then labels it with the number that is one less than the concealed digit. After his work receives teacher approval, he places it (unfolded) at a partner center.

Partner 1 selects a number fold-up and announces the featured two-digit number. Partner 2 states the numbers that are ten more and ten less; Partner 1 uses the flaps to check. Then the partners trade roles. They take turns with different number fold-ups as time allows.

Kate Gannon
Korn Elementary School
Durham, CT

Number & Operations

Chocolaty Place Value

Whet students' appetites for **place value** with this partner center. Place 12 red and 12 silver foil-wrapped chocolate candies in a container. Place the container, a pair of dice, the provided code, and half sheets of paper at a center.

Each partner divides his paper into fourths. To determine the first addend of a vertical addition problem, Partner 1 rolls the dice and takes this many red candies. He rolls again and takes this many silver candies. He uses the code to identify the corresponding number and then each partner writes it in the first section of his paper. Partner 2 uses the same process to determine the second addend. Each partner finishes setting up his problem and then solves it. The partners return the candies and continue the activity to complete their papers.

Code
red = ten
silver = one

Lin Attaya
Newton Rayzor Elementary
Denton, TX

Trading Places

Place-value practice is in the cards! At a center, place two place-value mats similar to the ones shown and a deck of playing cards (tens, jacks, queens, and jokers removed). Arrange for students to visit the center in pairs.

The players stack the cards facedown. Player 1 takes the top three cards one at a time, placing each card in the first empty column on his mat. If he has a king, he replaces it with another card from the stack and, if possible, rearranges two of his cards to create a larger number (aces represent one); he places the king in a discard pile. Player 2 takes a turn in a similar manner. The player with the greater three-digit number takes all the cards from the mats. Alternate play continues until only four cards remain in the draw pile. The player with more cards wins!

Liana Mahoney
Beaver River Central School
Beaver Falls, NY

79

Number & Operations

Place-Value Egg Baskets

Crack open students' **place-value** skills at this math center! Collect three baskets, an empty sterilized egg carton, and a dozen plastic eggs. Tuck cellophane grass in the baskets and label them as follows: "Hundreds," "Tens," and "Ones." Number the eggs and 12 paper strips from 1 to 12. Write a three-digit numeral on each paper strip and underline one digit per numeral. Create an answer key like the one shown. Place the labeled strips in the corresponding eggs and store the eggs in the egg carton. Place the baskets, the carton of eggs, and the answer key at a center. A student cracks open each egg, reads the numeral inside, and identifies the value of the underlined digit. Then he returns the paper strip to the egg and sorts the egg into the appropriate basket. When all 12 eggs are sorted, he uses the answer key to check his work.

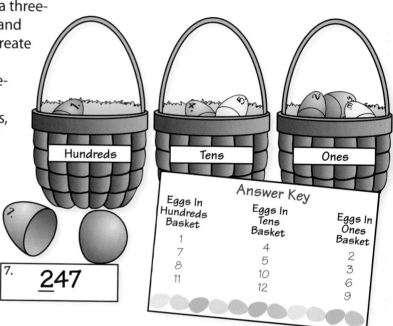

7. <u>2</u>47

Answer Key

Eggs In Hundreds Basket	Eggs In Tens Basket	Eggs In Ones Basket
1		
7	4	
8	5	2
11	10	3
	12	6
		9

All Clear!

Strategy and **addition** skills come into play with this partner game. Divide two sentence strip lengths into 8 sections and then number the sections on each strip. Place the strips, a supply of counters, and a pair of dice at a center. To begin, each player sets one counter in each section of her sentence strip. Player 1 rolls the dice and announces the numbers. She removes the counter from one or both of the corresponding sections on her sentence strip, or she removes the counter from the section that shows the total of her dice. Player 2 takes a turn in a similar manner. As alternate play continues, if a player cannot remove any counters for the numbers rolled, her turn is over. The first player to remove all of her counters wins.

adapted from an idea by Amy B. Barsanti
Pines Elementary
Plymouth, NC

Laying Down the Facts

This partner game is well-suited for **addition!** At a center, place a deck of playing cards with the face cards removed. One player deals six cards each to herself and her partner. She stacks the remaining cards facedown. To take a turn, a player studies her cards to determine whether she can represent an addition fact with three of them (jokers stand for zero and aces for one). If she can, she arranges the three cards on the playing surface and states the fact. Then she sets the cards aside and draws three cards (or as many as possible if three cards are not left in the stack). If she cannot represent a fact, she draws one card and her turn ends. Players alternate turns until they cannot represent any more facts. The player who puts aside more cards wins.

Shannon Adams
Waxahachie Faith Family Academy
Waxahachie, TX

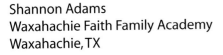

A.
5 + 3 = 8
3 + 5 = 8
8 − 5 = 3
8 − 3 = 5

B.
1 + 4 = 5
4 + 1 = 5
5 − 1 = 4
5 − 4 = 1

C.
6 + 2 = 8
2 + 6 = 8
8 − 2 = 6
8 − 6 = 2

D.
2 + 3 = 5
3 + 2 = 5
5 − 2 = 3
5 − 3 = 2

Fact-Family Fun

Now you can deliver **fact-family** practice at a moment's notice! Place a container of dominoes, drawing paper, and pencils at a center. A student folds a sheet of paper in half twice, unfolds the paper, and letters the four resulting boxes from A to D. To complete each box, he selects and illustrates a domino. He writes the two numbers from the domino as an addition fact and supplies the answer. Then he writes the three remaining number sentences in this fact family. Now that adds up to a whole lot of family fun!

Trudy White
Mayflower Elementary
Mayflower, AR

Number & Operations

Fishing for Fact Families

Reel in **fact families** at this math center! Label each of four fish cutouts with the numbers of a different fact family. Laminate the cutouts and then use a permanent marker to program the back of each one for self-checking. Place the fish, a supply of blank paper, pencils, crayons, and scissors at a center. A student draws four fish on her paper and copies a different fact family on each one. Then, in individual bubbles above each fish, she writes the math sentences for that family. After she checks her work, she colors the underwater scene and, if desired, trims the top of her paper to resemble waves.

Debbie Hicks
White Plains Elementary
Mount Airy, NC

Families of Facts

Help students feel right at home with **fact families!** On each of several paper triangles, write each number of a fact family in a separate corner. Store the triangles in a resealable plastic bag. Place the bag, and copies of the fact-family sheet on page 99 at a center. A student removes a triangle, writes the numbers on the roof of his first house, and then writes the corresponding fact family in the provided spaces. He uses two additional triangles to complete his paper.

adapted from an idea by Elizabeth Roberts
Manor Elementary
Levittown, PA

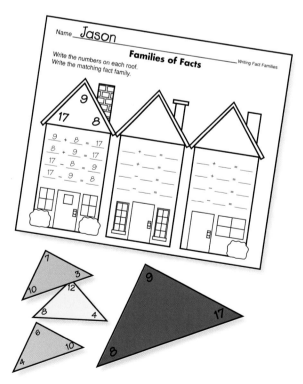

Number & Operations

All Aflutter!

Watch your students' knowledge of **math facts** take flight with these colorful fliers. Using the patterns on page 100, duplicate a desired number of butterfly bodies and wings on colorful construction paper. Program each butterfly body with a different sum or difference; then program a set of wings with corresponding math facts. Laminate and cut out the shapes. Use a permanent marker to program the backs of the wing cutouts for self-checking. Place the cutouts at a center with a supply of scratch paper (for calculating math facts). A student matches a pair of wings to each butterfly body, then peeks under each wing to check his work. Now that's a flock of fancy fliers!

Cindy Corey
Lealman Avenue Elementary
St. Petersburg, FL

Star Puzzlers

This star-studded **math fact** review is a bright idea! Duplicate the patterns on page 101 onto yellow construction paper—one copy for each star. To review math facts, program each star's center with a different answer; then program each set of star points with corresponding math facts. Cut out the patterns; then program the backs of the cutouts for self-checking. Store the cutouts in a resealable plastic bag at a center. A student assembles the stars, then flips the cutouts to check his work.

Maricela Perez
Anthon Elementary School
Uvalde, TX

Number & Operations

Salad Bowl Facts

Create an appetite for **math-fact** practice with a one-of-a-kind tossed salad. Using the patterns on page 102, create a supply of salad ingredients. For addition or multiplication fact practice, label the ingredients with numerals from 0 through 10 (or 12). For subtraction fact practice, label the ingredients with numerals from 0 through 18. Then laminate and cut out the shapes. Place the cutouts in a large, nonbreakable salad bowl. Display the salad bowl, a pair of salad tongs, paper plates, pencils, and blank paper at a center. A student uses the tongs to put a serving of salad on a paper plate. Then, using the numerals on her salad ingredients, she writes on her paper the addition, subtraction, or multiplication facts that she can make. The student then returns her serving of salad to the bowl and answers the math facts on her paper. If time allows, she may serve herself another helping of salad!

Angela Choate
Mustang Trails Elementary
Mustang, OK

Input and Output Well

Wishing for a center that features **addition and subtraction** in function tables? Try this partner activity! To make a well for the center, illustrate a 4" x 14" piece of construction paper, as shown, and then staple the ends together to form a cylinder. Place the well, copies of a blank function table, a 9" x 12" piece of felt (or another noise-reducing workmat), pennies, paper, and pencils at a center. Partner 1 stands the well on the felt. She gently drops a selected number of pennies into the well and then records the number in the input column. Partner 2 secretly chooses an addition rule such as "Add five." She places the appropriate number of pennies in the well, keeping them from her partner's view. Next, Partner 1 lifts the well and puts it aside. She counts the total number of pennies and writes this number in the output column. The activity continues until the function table is complete. Then Partner 1 studies the table, identifies the rule, and writes it on the recording sheet. The partners switch roles and repeat the activity.

adapted from an idea by Monica Cavender
Winstead, CT

Fact-Filled Foliage

Students rake in **addition and subtraction** practice at this "tree-mendous" center. Cut two large-branched tree trunks from brown tagboard. Label one trunk "odd" and the other "even." Use the leaf patterns on page 103 to make a number of construction paper leaves. Program each leaf with an unsolved addition or subtraction fact. For self-checking, label the back of each leaf with the answer and then mark it with an "X" if it is an odd number. Store the leaves in a decorated envelope. Place the trunks and envelope at a center stocked with paper and pencils. A student copies and completes each fact on a sheet of paper and then places the leaf on the appropriate tree. She flips the leaves to check her work.

Patricia Bedi
Hamilton Terrace School
Berkeley Heights, NJ

Leaves on odd tree: 3+6, 5+4, 10+7, 12+5
Leaves on even tree: 12-6, 8-8, 11-3
Bottom leaves: 12+7, 15-9

odd

even

Monster Math

Students will have a monstrously good time at this **addition and subtraction** center! Make five copies of the "Draw a Monster" form on page 104. Number each form and program it with desired math facts. Mount each programmed form on a slightly larger piece of construction paper. Place the forms, drawing paper, scrap paper (for math calculations), crayons or markers, and pencils at a center. A student chooses a "Draw a Monster" form. As he draws his monster, he refers to the form to find out how many arms, feet, noses, and so on his monster should have. Then he colors his creation.

Sr. Margaret Ann Wooden
St. Joseph's School
Martinsburg, WV

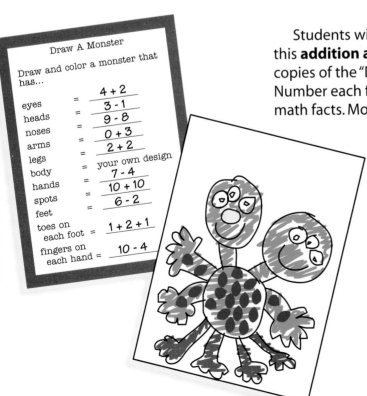

Draw A Monster

Draw and color a monster that has...

eyes	=	4 + 2
heads	=	3 - 1
noses	=	9 - 8
arms	=	0 + 3
legs	=	2 + 2
body	=	your own design
hands	=	7 - 4
spots	=	10 + 10
feet	=	6 - 2
toes on each foot	=	1 + 2 + 1
fingers on each hand	=	10 - 4

Number & Operations

Mouthwatering Math

Sweeten your students' **basic fact recall** at this pick-of-the-patch center. Copy and cut out several watermelon slices (patterns on page 105) and cut out a supply of paper seeds. Program each slice with a different math fact answer. Then, for each slice, label five or six seeds with corresponding math facts. Code the backs of the cutouts for self-checking and store them in a resealable plastic bag. Place the bag and one paper plate per watermelon slice in a basket. Set the basket at a center. A student lays each watermelon slice on a paper plate. Then she arranges the seeds on the corresponding slices. To check her work, she flips the seed cutouts.

Lisa Strieker
St. Paul Elementary
Highland, IL

High-Flying Computation

Get **computation** practice off the ground with this idea! Arrange several blank cards on a sheet of tagboard to represent hot-air balloon baskets. Illustrate a balloon above each basket. Draw lines from the balloons to the baskets. Then remove the cards and laminate the resulting workmat. Program each card with a math problem and use a wipe-off marker to label the balloons with the answers. Place the cards, workmat, paper, and pencils at a center.

A child selects a card, solves the math problem on his paper, and then places the card below the corresponding balloon. If he doesn't see his answer, he checks his computation. He repeats this process for the remaining problems. To vary the problems, prepare a new set of cards and reprogram the balloons.

adapted from an idea by Jennifer Nelson
Jacksonville, FL

Penguin Pals

This **addition and subtraction** math review is cool! Color and cut out four copies of the penguin patterns on page 106. Label each cutout with a math problem to solve. Number the cutouts, and then program the back of each one for self-checking. Place the cutouts, pencils, and a supply of blank paper at a center. A student folds her paper in half three times and then unfolds it and numbers the eight resulting boxes. (See the illustration.) After she solves each problem in its corresponding box, she flips the cutout to check her work.

Penney Dyer
Madison Primary
Madison, VA

Computation Cards

At this easy-to-prepare center, **two-digit addition** is in the cards! Stock a center with paper, pencils, a calculator, and a deck of playing cards (tens and face cards removed). A student takes four cards and arranges them faceup in two rows as shown. Using any aces as ones, he copies the corresponding digits onto a sheet of paper to create an addition problem. He solves the problem and uses the calculator to check his answer. Then he places the cards in a discard pile. He repeats the activity as time allows, reshuffling the cards as needed. To create a more challenging center, have each student use six cards at a time to practice three-digit addition.

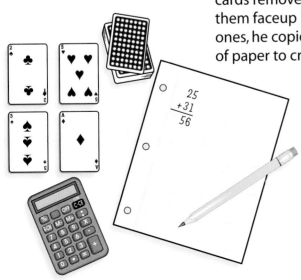

Angela Dunn
MetroWest Elementary
Orlando, FL

Colorful Computation

Watch **computation** skills take shape with this idea! Copy and cut out the hundred chart on page 107. Color selected boxes on the chart to make a desired design or a simple picture. To establish a color code for the image, list the appropriate colors as column headings on a sheet of paper. For each colored box, write a corresponding math problem in the correct column (see the sample). Then tuck the prepared hundred chart inside a large envelope. Mount the code on the front of the envelope. Place the envelope, copies of uncolored hundred charts, crayons, paper, and pencils at a center.

A student solves each math problem on a sheet of paper. For each problem, she colors the corresponding box on a hundred chart as indicated. She compares her completed paper to the one in the envelope to check her work.

Carol B. Everhart
Granite Quarry School
Spencer, NC

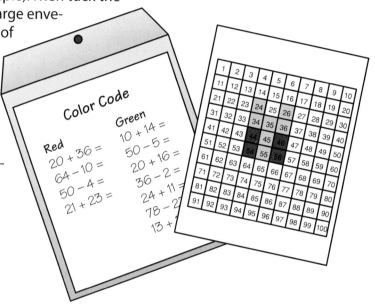

Color Code

Red

Green

$20 + 36 =$ $10 + 14 =$

$64 - 10 =$ $50 - 5 =$

$50 - 4 =$ $20 + 16 =$

$21 + 23 =$ $36 - 2 =$

$24 + 11$

$78 - 2$

$13 +$

All in the Family

Give **word-problem** practice a personal touch! Stock a center with paper, pencils, crayons, and a binder that contains a student supply of plastic page protectors. A student writes and illustrates a word problem that features one or more members of her family. She solves the problem on the back of her paper and then slides her paper into an empty page protector inside the notebook. When every student has a word problem in the binder, have students return to the center to solve the problems.

adapted from an idea by Natalie Fisher
West Side Montessori Center
Toledo, OH

Dad bakes 30 cookies.
Stevie Hall eats 10 cookies.
Olivia Hall eats 6 cookies.
Todd Hall eats 8 cookies.
How many cookies are left?

Pasta With Pizzazz

This partner **computation** center has plenty of "pasta-bilities"! Fill a plastic bowl with three or more different kinds of uncooked pasta shapes. Attach a sample of each pasta shape to a length of laminated tagboard labeled "Pasta Values." Then, using a wipe-off marker, write a desired number value beside each piece of pasta. Place the resulting pasta code, the bowl of pasta, a small scoop, paper napkins, and a supply of blank paper at a center. Each student places a scoop of pasta on a napkin and uses the code to determine its total value. Next he trades pasta with his partner and repeats the activity. The two students then compare their pasta totals. If their totals match, they return the pasta to the bowl. If one or both of the totals do not match, the students together recalculate the value of the pasta scoop(s). To keep the center fresh, reprogram the pasta code each week!

Gina Parisi
Demarest Elementary
Bloomfield, NJ

Hurray for Arrays!

Modeling **multiplication** builds a solid understanding of the multiplication concept. Label a class supply of cards with different fact problems. Place the cards, cereal pieces, glue, crayons, and sturdy paper at a center. A student selects a fact card. Then she makes and labels an array that models the problem and reveals its answer.

Sally Wallace
O'Neill Elementary
O'Neill, NE

Gracie

$3 \times 5 = 15$

$3 \times 5 =$

Chilly Computation

This cool partner game provides a solid review of **basic multiplication** facts. Vertically position an empty ice cube tray. Use self-adhesive dots to label the top of each section with a number that is appropriate for multiplication practice. Place the tray, two small pom-poms, paper, and pencils at a center.

The players position the tray so that the numbers face Player 2. To play one round, Player 1 closes his eyes and randomly drops each pom-pom into a different section. He turns the tray to view the numbers and then multiplies them. He writes his answer and removes the pom-poms. Then Player 2 takes a turn. The player with the greater answer earns one point. (No points are awarded for a tie.) After a total of ten rounds, the top-scoring player is declared the winner.

adapted from an idea by Tracy Abernathy
Chatsworth Elementary
Chatsworth, GA

Basic-Facts Blossoms

Create a colorful garden of **multiplication** facts review. Use the patterns on page 108 to make an equal number of construction paper flower blossoms and centers. Label each flower center with a different product. Then, for each flower center, program a blossom with one or two variations of its problem (see the illustration). Laminate the cutouts for durability and cut them out. For self-checking, code the back of each blossom with its corresponding product. Store the cutouts in a plastic bag at a center. A student matches each flower center to a flower blossom. Then she flips the blossoms to check her work.

Shannon D. Matthews
Lake View Academy
Oklahoma City, OK

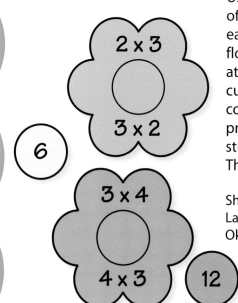

Number & Operations

Four in a Row

Students will have their **multiplication** facts covered with this partner game! In a center, place a multiplication chart, a deck of playing cards (face cards removed), and a supply of game markers in two different colors. Arrange for students to visit the center in pairs.

Player 1 stacks the cards facedown and then takes the top two cards. Using any aces as ones, she states the product. Player 2 uses the multiplication chart to check her answer. If the answer is correct, Player 1 places a game marker on a corresponding chart space. If the answer is not correct or none of the corresponding spaces are free, her turn is over. The game continues with players alternating roles. The first player to cover four spaces in a horizontal, vertical, or diagonal row wins!

Stephanie Scandalito
St. Mary Academy
Port Huron, MI

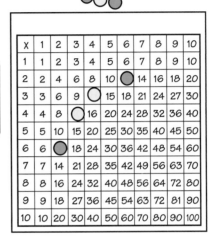

Egg Carton Multiplication

Do your students need "eggs-tra" practice with **multiplication** facts? Try this! Number 12 sticky dots with desired factors and press one sticky dot into each egg cup of a sterilized egg carton. Place the prepared carton, two pom-poms, paper, and pencils at a center. A student drops the pom-poms inside the egg carton, closes the lid, and gently shakes the carton. Then she opens the carton and on her paper writes (in the form of a multiplication problem) the factors where the pom-poms landed. Then she solves the fact, closes the carton, and repeats the activity until she's written and answered a designated number of facts.

adapted from an idea by Amy Barsanti
Pines Elementary School
Plymouth, NC

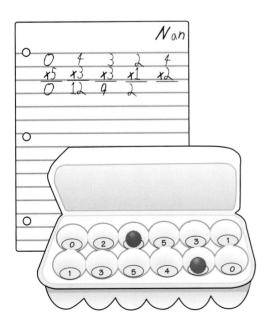

Number & Operations

Multiplication Minibooks

These tiny booklets provide **multiplication** practice in a big way! Stock a center with a stapler, marker, and pencils. Also provide 3" x 12" construction paper strips (booklet covers) and paper strips that are approximately 2" x 5½" (booklet pages). A student folds a construction paper strip in half and staples several paper strips inside. She uses a marker to title and sign her resulting booklet as desired.

Next, she folds back the ends of the pages as a group and then unfolds them. She labels the front of each page with a multiplication fact that she needs to practice, writing the problem to the left of the fold line and the product to the right. She folds back each product so that its page can be turned separately. She reads a problem, identifies the product, and then unfolds the page to check the answer.

adapted from an idea by Terri Hamilton
Chariho Schools
Wood River Junction, RI

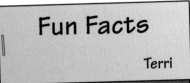

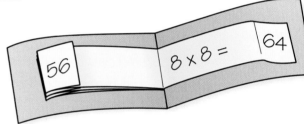

Delectable Division

Candy eggs lend a manipulative flair to this tasty **division** center. Partially fill five disposable bowls with cellophane grass, and fill an additional bowl with 30 foil-covered chocolate eggs. Also label a set of colorful, egg-shaped cutouts with division facts that have a divisor of five or less, and a dividend of 30 or less. (Depending on your students' abilities, include some problems with remainders.) Program the cutouts for self-checking and laminate them for durability. Place the bowls and the egg cutouts at a center. A student selects a cutout, reads the fact, and sets out as many grass-filled bowls as the divisor. To solve the fact, she takes the dividend in candy eggs and divides the eggs equally into the bowls. She places any leftover eggs (the remainder) to the side. Then she flips the cutout to check her work. If her answer is correct, she places the candy eggs back into their bowl. If her answer is incorrect, she adjusts her candy calculation before she returns the candy. The student continues in this manner until each division fact has been solved.

Amy Polcyn
South Lyon Community Schools
South Lyon, MI

Number & Operations

Pocket Change

Bank on improved **coin-counting** skills at this easy-to-adapt center. Mount ten library pockets onto a sheet of poster board. Number the tops of ten vertically positioned index cards 1 to 10. Below each number, stamp a different coin combination that is suitable for students' ability levels. Label an index card half for each total and use a paper clip to attach it to a pocket as shown. Place the prepared poster board, the coin-combination cards, and an answer key at a center.

A student selects a card, counts the coins, and places the card in the corresponding pocket. He repeats the process with the remaining cards and then uses the answer key to check his work. As students' coin-counting skills progress, prepare more challenging cards and label the pockets with the corresponding totals.

Anne E. South
East Oro Public School
Orillia, Ontario, Canada

Cashing In

Money-counting skills are sure to profit at this partner center! Label the lids of an even number of empty film canisters with different money amounts. In a separate container place quarters, dimes, nickels, and pennies that can be used to make each money amount. Place the container of coins, the canisters, and a felt square at a center. Partner 1 selects a canister, places coins inside it that equal the programmed amount, and passes the canister to his partner. Partner 2 pours the coins onto the felt square and verifies the count. After the coins and empty canister are returned to their original locations, Partner 2 selects a different canister and the process is repeated. The partners continue in this manner until the coins in each canister have been counted and verified.

Nell Roberts
The Covenant School
Charlottesville, VA

Number & Operations

Saving for a Snowy Day!

Cash in on **money-counting** skills with this center activity! Using the pattern on page 109, duplicate a supply of snow pals. Label each pattern with a different combination of coins using coin stickers, paper coins, or a stamp pad and a set of coin stamps. For added appeal, color the hats and scarves. Then laminate and cut out the snow pals. Use a permanent marker to program the back of each cutout for self-checking. A student calculates the total value of the coins shown on each snow pal, then flips the cutout to check his work.

Mary Taylor
Sun Prairie, WI

56¢

A Real Deal!

To reinforce **money** skills and **problem-solving** skills, clip a supply of coupons from magazines and newspapers; then attach each coupon to a 3" x 9" strip of construction paper. Choose a coin combination that equals the face value of the featured coupon and attach one sticky dot to the strip for each coin in the combination. Code the backs of the strips for self-checking; then place the coupon strips and a supply of coin manipulatives at a center. A student chooses a coupon strip; then he determines a combination of coins that equals the face value of the coupon and uses one coin for each dot on the strip. To check his work, he flips the strip over. The student continues in this manner until he has completed each coupon strip.

Pat Rutland
Stockdale Elementary
Stockdale, TX

75¢

75¢ Off
Any Pa

75¢

50¢

50¢ Off

50¢

50¢

50¢

35¢

35¢ OFF
TEDDY BERRIES CEREAL

Teddy
BERRIES

35¢

35¢

35¢

Number & Operations

Let's Go Shopping!

This **coin-counting** center is sure to get students' stamp of approval! At a center, place coin stamps, a stamp pad, and a supply of unwanted or expired coupons that show discounts less than $1.00. Also provide white paper, glue, scissors, and pencils. A child visually divides her paper in half. She glues two coupons near the top of each half. For each pair of coupons, she writes the total savings. Then she stamps the fewest coin impressions possible to show the corresponding amount.

adapted from an idea by Connie Craig
Troy Elementary Center East
Troy, PA

On the Money

Students cash in on **equivalent coin amounts** with this "cent-sational" game! Arrange a supply of imitation coins on a sterilized foam tray. Place the tray, a die, and two laminated hand cutouts at a center. Arrange for students to visit the center in pairs. In turn, each player rolls the die. He takes the corresponding number of pennies and places them on his hand cutout. If he has five or six pennies, he exchanges five of them for a nickel. When he gets two nickels or ten pennies he trades them for a dime, and so on. Alternate play continues for a predetermined number of turns. The player with the greater total wins!

Eleanor Shill
Highlands Elementary
Winter Springs, FL

Coin Exchange

You can bank on accurate **coin exchanges** taking place at this partner center. Place a die and a container of imitation coins at a center. (For a game that concludes at 50¢, provide the following coins: ten pennies, three nickels, three dimes, three quarters, one half-dollar.) To play, partners take turns rolling the die. Each partner collects cents equal to the number he rolls. When a partner collects his coins, he evaluates his coin set. If he can exchange coins for a coin of greater value, he makes the trade. If a player overlooks a trade during his turn, his partner can point out the missed trade during his own turn and earn an extra roll of the die. The first player to collect 50¢ wins the game.

Anne M. Bosarge
Lyman Elementary School
Richmond Hill, GA

Math on the Menu

Dish up a healthy serving of **money computation** practice! At a center, place a take-out menu from a local restaurant, a calculator, drawing paper, crayons, and pencils. A student visually divides his paper into quarters. In the first section, he lists and illustrates two chosen menu items. Then he writes and solves an addition problem to find the total cost of his meal. He repeats this process in the remaining sections for three different meals. Finally, he uses the calculator to verify his dining expenses. Check, please!

Cheryl Sergi
Greene, NY

Number & Operations

Buggy Over Fractions

These adorable ladybugs make **fraction** practice a friendly experience. Enlarge the ladybug pattern on page 110 to a desired size; then duplicate ten copies of the pattern on red construction paper. Number the ladybug patterns from one to ten, and attach a different set of two colors of sticky dots to each ladybug. Cut out the patterns; then program the backs of the cutouts for self-checking. Store the ladybugs in a resealable plastic bag. Place the bag of cutouts, pencils, and a supply of paper at a center. A student numbers his paper from 1 to 10. For each ladybug, the student determines what fractional part of the dot set each color of dot represents. (For example, if there are two blue dots and four yellow dots, $\frac{2}{6}$ of the set is blue and $\frac{4}{6}$ of the set is yellow.) He writes his answers on his paper; then he flips the cutout to check his work. He continues in this manner until he has completed the center.

Mary Taylor
Sun Prairie, WI

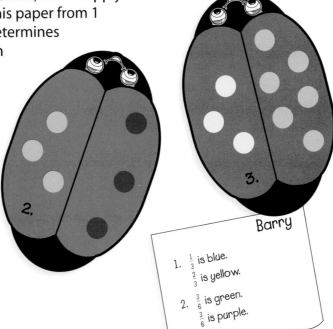

Barry

1. $\frac{1}{3}$ is blue.
   $\frac{2}{3}$ is yellow.

2. $\frac{3}{6}$ is green.
   $\frac{3}{6}$ is purple.

Jelly Bean Fractions

Reinforce **fractions** at this jelly bean center. Using only four jelly bean colors, place a small set of candies in each of three resealable plastic bags. Next, write the four colors on a copy of the recording sheet from page 110. Then place a supply of the prepared recording sheet in a center along with pencils and the bags of jelly beans. A student selects a bag and completes the provided activity. Encourage interested students to repeat the activity with each remaining bag of candy.

Kim Battista
Holland Hill School, Fairfield, CT

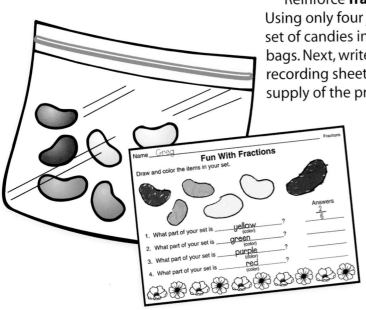

Number & Operations

Fishing for Fractions

Reel in plenty of **fraction** practice at this tasty math center! In a clean container, mix a six-ounce package of cheddar fish-shaped crackers with similarly sized packages of pretzel and pizza fish-shaped crackers. Make a cracker code like the one shown. Then place the code, the container of crackers, napkins, a ¼-cup measurer, pencils, and student copies of page 111 at a center. A student places one-quarter cup of crackers on an unfolded napkin. Next he sorts the crackers and completes the reproducible activity. When his work is finished, he eats his catch!

Melanie J. Miller
Nashport, OH

Cracker Code

Cheddar

Pizza

Pretzel

Name —

Flavorful Fractions

Math center
Fractions

1. Look at your bag of marshmallows.
   How many marshmallows do you think are in the bag?
   Write your estimate on the line. ___15___

2. Open your bag.
   Use crayons to graph your marshmallows by color.

	1	2	3	4	5	6	7	8
orange								
yellow								
pink								
green								

3. Use your graph. How many marshmallows of each color do you have?
   ___2___ orange ___3___ yellow ___4___ pink ___3___ green

4. How many marshmallows do you have in all? ___12___

5. In each box show how many marshmallows you have of that color.
   Use your crayons.

   orange   pink
   yellow   green

6. Study each box in Number 5. Write a fraction that describes it.

   $\frac{2}{12}$ = orange $\frac{3}{12}$ = yellow $\frac{4}{12}$ = pink $\frac{3}{12}$ = green

---

Flavorful Fractions

This math center makes learning about **fractions** a sweet treat! For each student, place 12 miniature flavored marshmallows in a resealable plastic bag, making certain that each bag contains all four colors and no more than eight of any one color. Store the bags in a decorated container; then place the container, crayons, pencils, and student copies of page 112 at a center. Each student chooses a bag of marshmallows from the container and uses it to complete the reproducible activity. After a student has had a classmate verify his work, he eats his marshmallows in fractional portions! Mmmm, that $^5/_{12}$ of marshmallows was delicious!

Pam Williams
Dixieland Elementary
Lakeland, FL

Word Bank

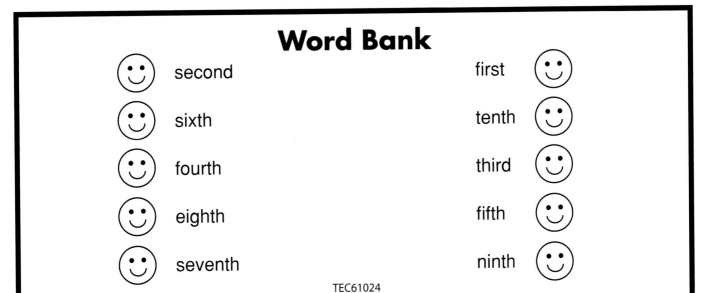

second   first

sixth   tenth

fourth   third

eighth   fifth

seventh   ninth

TEC61024

Name _____ Writing Fact Families

Families of Facts

Write the numbers on each roof.
Write the matching fact family.

©The Mailbox® • *Learning Centers* • TEC61024

Note to the teacher: Use with "Families of Facts" on page 82.

Butterfly Patterns

Use with "All Aflutter!" on page 83 and
"Beautiful Butterflies on page 127.

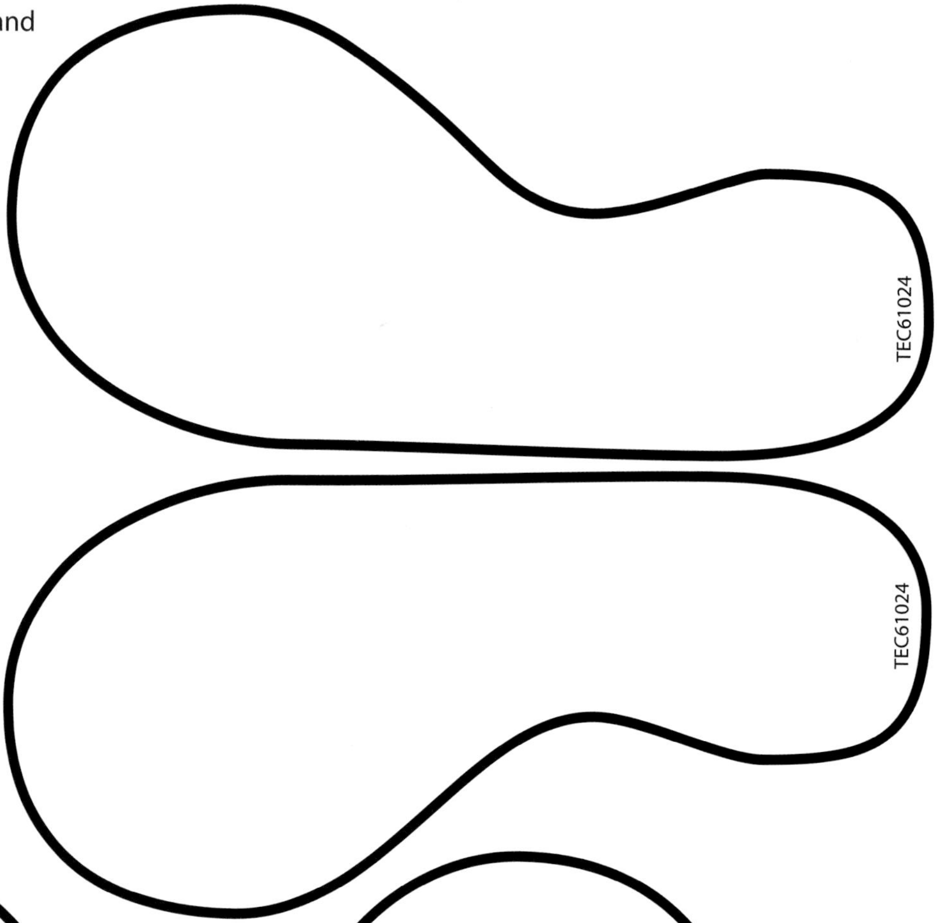

TEC61024

TEC61024

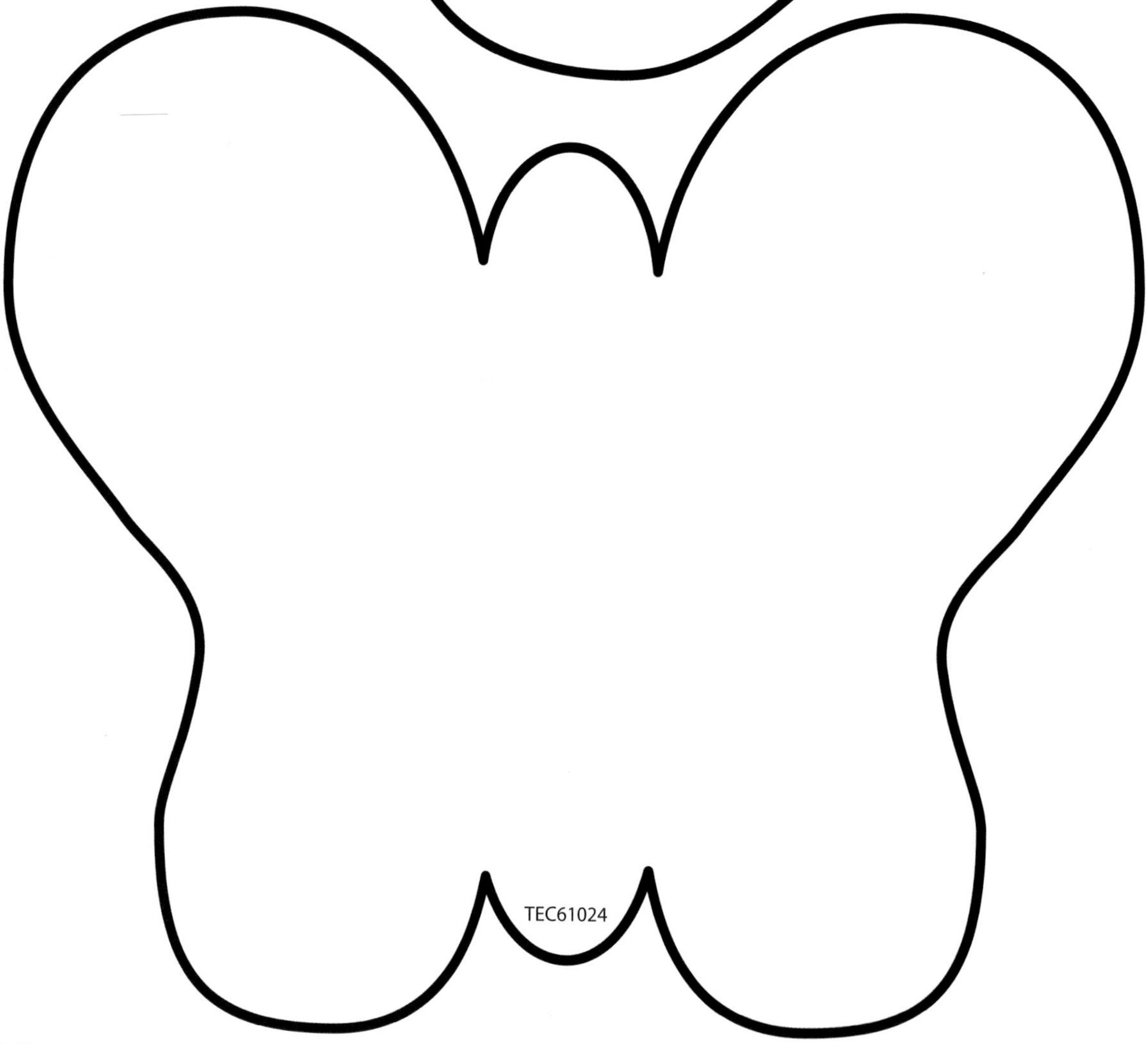

TEC61024

TEC61024

TEC61024

TEC61024

TEC61024

TEC61024

TEC61024

Salad Patterns

Use with "Salad Bowl Facts" on page 84.

Lettuce Duplicate on green construction paper.

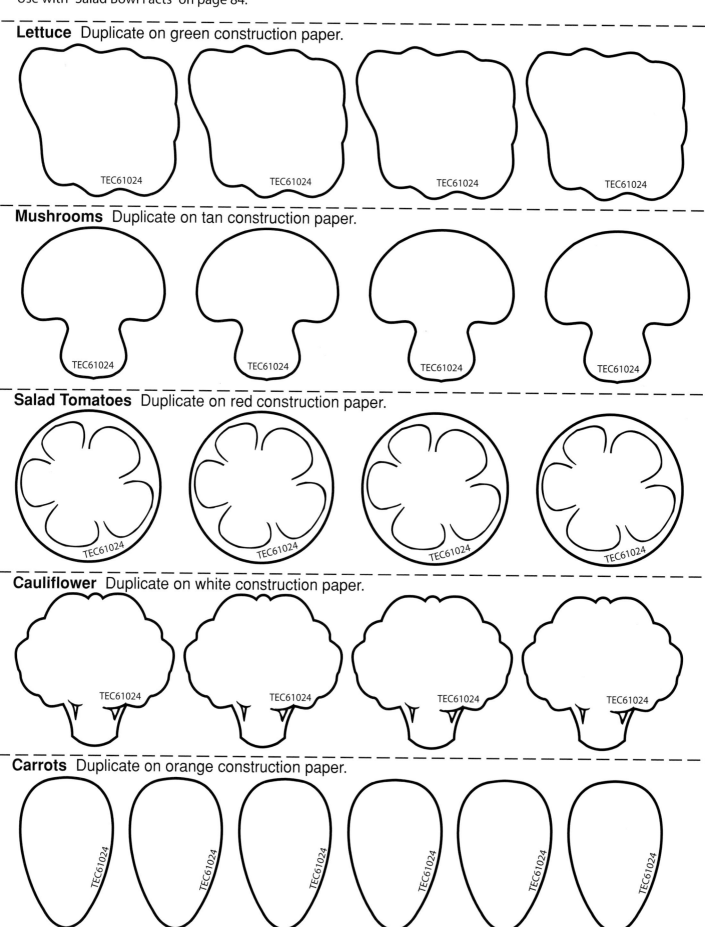

TEC61024 TEC61024 TEC61024 TEC61024

Mushrooms Duplicate on tan construction paper.

TEC61024 TEC61024 TEC61024 TEC61024

Salad Tomatoes Duplicate on red construction paper.

TEC61024 TEC61024 TEC61024 TEC61024

Cauliflower Duplicate on white construction paper.

TEC61024 TEC61024 TEC61024 TEC61024

Carrots Duplicate on orange construction paper.

TEC61024 TEC61024 TEC61024 TEC61024 TEC61024 TEC61024

Use with "Fact-Filled Foliage" on page 85 and "Leafy Linear Measurement" on page 115.

TEC61024

TEC61024

TEC61024

TEC61024

Draw a Monster

Draw and color a monster that has...

Eyes = _____

Heads = _____

Noses = _____

Arms = _____

Legs = _____

Body = Your own design

Hands = _____

Spots = _____

Feet = _____

Toes on each foot = _____

Fingers on each hand = _____

Note to the teacher: Use with "Monster Math" on page 85.

TEC61024

Ladybug Pattern

Use with "Buggy Over Fractions" on page 97.

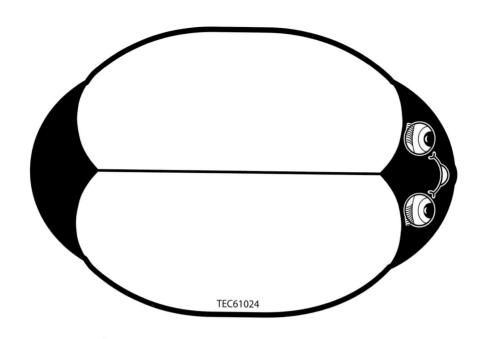

TEC61024

- -

Name_____

Fun With Fractions

Draw and color the items in your set.

Answers

1. What part of your set is _____?   _____
                                 (color)

2. What part of your set is _____?   _____
                                 (color)

3. What part of your set is _____?   _____
                                 (color)

4. What part of your set is _____?   _____
                                 (color)

Note to the teacher: Use with "Jelly Bean Fractions" on page 97.

Name _____

What a Catch!

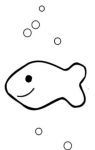

Sort your catch of fish crackers.
Write a number to answer each question.

1. How many crackers in your catch are pizza? _____
2. How many crackers in your catch are cheddar? _____
3. How many crackers in your catch are pretzel? _____
4. How many crackers did you catch in all? _____

Remember! The bottom number is the total number of crackers in your catch.

Use the information above.
Write a fraction to answer each question.

5. What part of your catch is pizza?

6. What part of your catch is cheddar?

7. What part of your catch is pretzel?

The top number describes a part of the crackers.

On the lines, write a comparative sentence about each cracker.
(For example: I have more pizza crackers than pretzel crackers.)

8. Pizza: _____
_____

9. Cheddar: _____
_____

10. Pretzel: _____
_____

For Fraction Experts Only!
Write a fraction to answer each question.

11. What part of your catch is pizza and cheddar?

12. What part of your catch is pretzel and pizza?

13. What part of your catch is cheddar and pretzel?

14. What part of your catch is not cheddar?

©The Mailbox® • *Learning Centers* • TEC61024

Note to the teacher: Use with "Fishing for Fractions" on page 98.

Flavorful Fractions

1. Look at your bag of marshmallows.
   How many marshmallows do you think are in the bag?
   Write your estimate on the line. _____

2. Open your bag.
   Use crayons to graph your marshmallows by color.

orange								
yellow								
pink								
green								
	1	2	3	4	5	6	7	8

3. Use your graph. How many marshmallows of each color do you have?

   _____ orange   _____ yellow   _____ pink   _____ green

4. How many marshmallows do you have in all? _____

5. In each box show how many marshmallows you have of that color.
   Use your crayons.

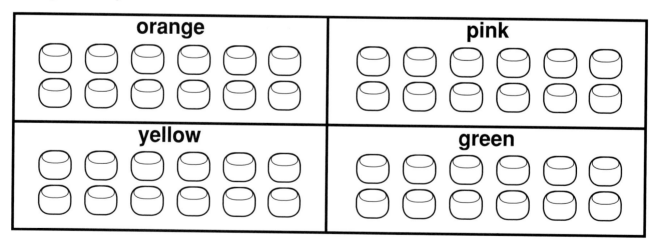

6. Study each box in Number 5. Write a fraction that describes it.

   $\dfrac{\Box}{\Box}$ = orange $\dfrac{\Box}{\Box}$ = yellow $\dfrac{\Box}{\Box}$ = pink $\dfrac{\Box}{\Box}$ = green

Note to the teacher: Use with "Flavorful Fractions" on page 98.

For Good Measure

Students size up their **measurement** skills at this center. On individual cards write measurement-related questions that can be solved in the classroom. Consider questions like "How many inches wide is the door?" and "Which weighs more—the red marker or the ruler?" Write student directions on a large card, and program the back of this card with an answer key. Place the question cards in a plastic two- or four-cup capacity container. Place the container, the direction card, a supply of paper, pencils, and the materials needed to answer the questions at a center. A student solves each measurement question and writes his answer on his paper. Then he uses the answer key to find out how his measurement skills measure up!

Tori Herrera
Cook Elementary
Goshen, OH

How many centimeters long is a chalkboard eraser?

Mark

1. 10 inches
2. The ruler is heavier.
3. 4 cm
4.

Name Karen

Chilly Measures

Measuring in Inches

My snow pal's name is Frosty

Here is how my snow pal measures up:

Hat = 2 inches
Top snowball = 2½ inches
Middle snowball = 3½ inches
Bottom snowball = 5 inches
Height = 12 inches

Chilly Measures

This center gives students plenty of opportunity to **measure in inches!** To prepare, cut a supply of white paper circles in various sizes. Place the circles, a class supply of 12" x 18" construction paper, and student copies of "Chilly Measures" on page 118 at a center. Also provide construction paper, glue, scissors, rulers, and pencils. A student glues three different-size circles on the construction paper to create a snow pal. She cuts out a paper hat from construction paper, glues it onto her snow pal, and adds desired details. Then she completes a recording sheet for her frosty friend, measuring to the nearest inch or half inch.

Cathy Ann Brandau
Orchard Hills Elementary
Novi, MI

Measurement

Fancy Footwork

At this **measurement** center place a supply of construction paper and writing paper, scissors, pencils, paper clips, and several task cards like the one shown. A student traces the outline of his shoe on construction paper and cuts out the resulting shape. Then he uses his cutout to complete the measurement tasks at hand. He records his answers on a sheet of writing paper. When he has completed all the measurement tasks, he clips his shoe cutout to his answer sheet.

Collect the students' work; then place the completed projects along with the task cards at the center the following week. Ask each student to choose one measurement project (other than his own) and use the provided cutout to check the recorded measurements.

Find two classroom items that equal the length of your shoe cutout.

Kelly A. Wong
Berlyn School
Diamond Bar, CA

Centimeter Snakes

This center is perfect for students to measure some colorful **centimeter** snakes. Cut 15 strips of paper into different centimeter lengths. Round the corners of each strip; then number the strips and decorate them as desired. Design an answer key that can be attached to the bottom of a cylindrical container. Tape the key to the bottom of the container; then store the centimeter snakes inside. Place the container, a centimeter ruler, a supply of paper, and pencils at a center. A student numbers her paper from 1 to 15; then she removes each snake, measures it, and records her centimeter measurement on her paper. When all of the snakes have been measured, she turns the can over and checks her work.

Rita Yanoff
Sussex Christian School
Hope, NJ

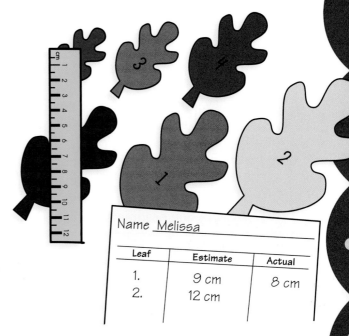

Measurement

Leafy Linear Measurement

Rake in **metric measurement** practice! Photocopy the leaf patterns on page 103 at several different percentages to make identically shaped leaves of various sizes. Number and cut out the leaves. Place the leaves and copies of a recording sheet similar to the one shown at a center stocked with a ruler. A student sequences the leaves from the shortest to the longest. She estimates the length of the first leaf to the nearest centimeter, writes her estimate, and then measures and writes the actual length. She repeats this process with each leaf, considering previous measurements to guide her estimates.

Janice Keer
Eagle Bluff School
Onalaska, WI

Name Melissa		
Leaf	Estimate	Actual
1.	9 cm	8 cm
2.	12 cm	

shorter	14cm	longer

Fishy Measurements

Students size up the day's catch at this center. Prepare several fish cutouts in a variety of **centimeter** lengths. Letter the fish and then place them in a pail. Label the pail with a length that is longer than about half of the fish. To make an answer key, list the fish by letter in groups to show which are shorter than, equal to, or longer than the designated length. Place the pail, the answer key, a metric ruler, and a supply of paper at a center.

A student divides his paper into three columns. He labels the middle column with the designated length and labels the first and third columns as shown. He measures each fish and writes its letter in the correct column. Then he uses the answer key to check his work.

adapted from an idea by Linda Stroik
Bannach Elementary School
Stevens Point, WI

Measurement

Scheduling Time

Here's a kid-pleasing activity that integrates **telling time** and writing. Place a clock stamp, a stamp pad, pencils, crayons, and a supply of blank paper at a center. A student titles her paper "A Perfect Saturday" and then stamps a column of clock faces down the left edge of the paper as shown. She programs the first clock to show the time she'll get out of bed. To the right of the clock she writes the matching digital time in crayon, and then she uses a pencil to describe what she plans to do at that time. She programs and labels the remaining clocks on her paper to show the activities she'd schedule for her perfect day. Display the completed schedules and plenty of time-related conversations will follow!

Stacie Stone Davis
Lima, NY

A Perfect Saturday

8:30 — Get out of bed.

9:00 — Have pancakes with Dad and go to the pet store.

11:00 — Play with Spencer at the park.

7:00 — Have ice cream with my big brother and his girlfriend.

10:00 — Go to bed.

by Kally

In a Day's Time

Schedule this opportunity to boost **time-telling** skills. Place a class supply of 3" x 12" construction paper strips and copies of the clock patterns on page 118 at a center. A child illustrates each clock to show the time of a typical school day activity and then writes a corrresponding sentence. Next, she cuts the sections apart and stacks them in order. She folds a construction paper strip in half, staples the pages inside, and titles the booklet "My School Day."

adapted from an idea by Janice Driscoll
Midlakes Intermediate School
Clifton Springs, NY

I eat lunch at 12:30 every day.

Measurement

Time Rolls On

Challenge capable students with this advanced **time-telling** activity! Place a clock stamp, a stamp pad, pencils, a pair of dice, and a supply of paper at a center. A student stamps a clock face on his paper. To program the clock, he rolls the dice and draws the minute hand to the number that matches the sum of his roll. To determine the hour, he tallies a second roll of the dice. Then he draws the hour hand on the clock face, making sure that its placement corresponds with the minutes shown. Below the clock he writes the corresponding digital time. The student continues in this manner as time allows. Ticktock, ticktock!

Jennifer VonPinnon
Eastwood Elementary
West Fargo, ND

"The School Times"

Time keeps on ticking at this center—**elapsed time,** that is! Stock the center with 5" x 6" pieces of drawing paper (five per student) and 6" x 10" pieces of newspaper (one per student). Also provide discarded newspapers, scissors, glue, pencils, a black marker, and a stapler. A student cuts out five examples of time spans from the discarded newspapers and glues each example on a piece of drawing paper. On the back of the paper, she writes how much time elapses during the time span. Next she folds a 6" x 10" piece of newspaper in half and uses the marker to write "The [school name] Times" and her byline on the front of the resulting booklet cover. She stacks the five pages she has created, keeping the time spans faceup, and staples the stack inside the cover.

The following week, provide additional practice with elapsed time by featuring these hot-off-the-press booklets at the center. For each booklet a student reads, she calculates the elapsed time in each featured time span and then turns the page to check her work.

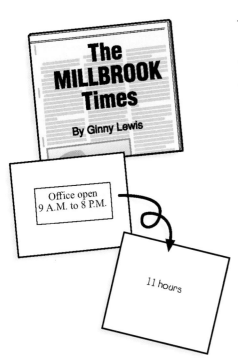

Mary Ann Lewis
Tallahassee, FL

Clock Patterns

Use with "In a Day's Time" on page 116.

TEC61024

TEC61024

TEC61024

TEC61024

Name _____

Chilly Measures

My snow pal's name is _____.

Here is how my snow pal measures up:

Hat = _____

Top snowball = _____

Middle snowball = _____

Bottom snowball = _____

Height = _____

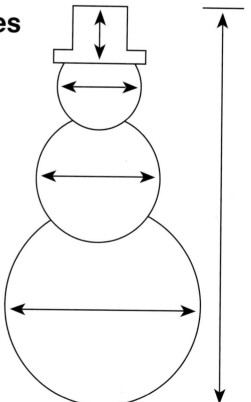

©The Mailbox® • *Learning Centers* • TEC61024

Note to the teacher: Use the recording sheet with "Chilly Measures" on page 113.

Where in the World?

Reinforce **geography and map skills** all year long! Place paper; pencils; and a desired map, atlas, or globe at a center along with a laminated poster titled "Where in the world is _____?" Each week use a wipe-off marker to write a different location in the blank and to program the poster with one or more questions about it. Using the provided resource, a student finds the mystery location. Then, on his paper, he describes where it is and answers each question about it. Invite interested students to further investigate this location.

Kate Pointkowski
Spring Hill Elementary School
McLean, VA

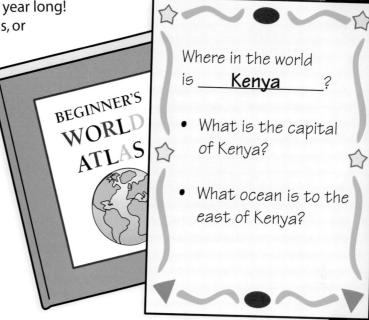

Where in the world is ___Kenya___?

- What is the capital of Kenya?

- What ocean is to the east of Kenya?

Todd

Africa is bigger than North America.

Map Match

This idea helps students take note of **geographic locations!** Display a world map. Use small sticky notes to make two identical labels for each of several familiar continents, countries, or bodies of water. For each location, place one label atop the other; adhere the labels to the map. Set a globe and paper at the center. A student removes one label from a chosen location (leaving the second label in place) and uses it to mark the same location on the globe. He repeats this process with the remaining places. Then, for each place, he writes a sentence about its location or relative size. To prepare the center for another student, he removes the labels from the globe and returns them to the map.

Geoff Mihalenko
Harry S. Truman Elementary
Parlin, NJ

Social Studies

Traveling With Writing

Here's a first-class idea for linking **geography** and writing! Request used bus, train, or airline ticket stubs from parents. Store the stubs in a plastic bag. Place the bag, writing paper, pencils, and selected maps at a center. A child studies a chosen ticket stub and identifies the place of departure and the destination. He locates these two places on a map. Then, using the chosen stub for inspiration, he writes about an imaginary journey to the indicated destination or what he did once he arrived there.

Sonya Franklin
Springville Elementary
Springdale, AL

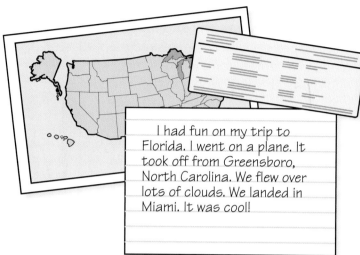

I had fun on my trip to Florida. I went on a plane. It took off from Greensboro, North Carolina. We flew over lots of clouds. We landed in Miami. It was cool!

Provides Services

Good or Service?

Keep a lid on **goods and services!** Use Con-Tact paper to cover two boxes and their lids. Assemble the boxes and label one "Provides Goods" and the other "Provides Services." Then make five one-inch slits in each lid as shown. Cut out the cards and the answer key on page 125. Hot-glue each card to one end of a craft stick. Place the cards, answer key, boxes, and a supply of paper at a center. A student displays each community helper in the lid of the appropriate box. On her paper she lists the helpers in each box along with the goods or services they provide. Then she uses the answer key to check her work.

Laura Mihalenko
Harry S. Truman Elementary
Parlin, NJ

| Police Officer | Farmer | Doctor | Baker | Mail Carrier |
| Artist | Hairstylist | Author | Firefighter | Carpenter |

Answer Key

Provides Goods	**Goods Provided** *(Answers will vary.)*	**Provides Services**	**Services Provided** *(Answers will vary.)*
Farmer	fruits and vegetables	Police Officer	safety
Baker	baked items	Doctor	health care
Artist	pictures	Mail Carrier	mail delivery
Carpenter	houses	Hairstylist	hair care
Author	books	Firefighter	fire safety

TEC61024   TEC61024   TEC61024   TEC61024   TEC61024

TEC61024   TEC61024   TEC61024   TEC61024   TEC61024

TEC61024

A Colorful Connection

Students warm right up to this art center. Stock a center with a color wheel, 7" x 7" drawing paper, 3" x 8" strips of writing paper, 9" x 12" sheets of construction paper, crayons, pencils, and glue. A student uses only warm colors (red, orange, yellow, or some combination of these colors) to render an illustration on drawing paper. On writing paper he describes his illustration and how it makes him feel. Then he glues his work onto a sheet of construction paper as shown.

Emily Navidad
Morganton Road Elementary School
Fayetteville, NC

My picture is of the desert. It makes me feel very hot and thirsty. But I think the snake likes the hot sun!

by Gary

Beautiful Butterflies

With a flit and flutter, recycle construction paper scraps and bring the beauty of butterflies into your classroom! Enlarge the butterfly pattern on page 100 to a desired size; then duplicate student copies on white construction paper. Place the copies, scissors, glue, a hole puncher, and a supply of construction paper scraps at a center. A student cuts out a butterfly; then he snips and punches a collection of colorful construction paper scraps. Next the student glues the pieces atop his butterfly cutout until it is covered with colorful clippings and attaches a pair of construction paper antennae. Now that's a one-of-a-kind fancy flier!

Art Extravaganza

Recycle materials at this art center, which is long on usability and short on preparation time. Gather together leftover or ready-to-discard greeting cards, wallpaper samples, construction paper and gift-wrap scraps, buttons, stickers, canceled stamps, and other recyclable materials. Sort them into containers at a center that you've equipped with glue, scissors, crayons, 12" x 18" sheets of construction paper, and other desired art supplies. A student uses the materials at the center to create an original piece of artwork.

Keepsake Quilt Patches

The focus of this art center is favorite memories from the school year! Place 9-inch squares of drawing paper and 12-inch squares of colorful construction paper at a center along with crayons, a black marker, and glue. A student folds a square of drawing paper in half twice; then he unfolds the paper and draws and labels four favorite memories—one in each section. He mounts his artwork on construction paper and uses the black marker to write his name near the bottom of his resulting quilt patch. If desired, display the completed projects as a class quilt. Then send each child home with his keepsake on the last day of the school year.

adapted from an idea by Shirley Freeland
Jefferson Parkway Elementary
Newnan, GA